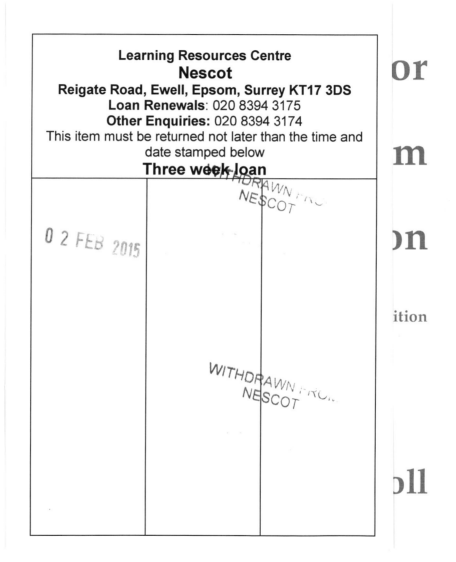
or

m

on

ition

oll

Oxford Centre for Staff and Learning Development

© Oxford Centre for Staff and Learning Development 2007

Published by
THE OXFORD CENTRE FOR STAFF AND LEARNING DEVELOPMENT
Oxford Brookes University
Headington
Oxford
OX3 0BP

A Handbook for Deterring Plagiarism in Higher Education
(2nd Edition)
ISBN   1-873576-74-9
         978-1-873576-74-8

British Library Cataloguing-in-Publication Data.
A catalogue record for this book is available from the British Library.

Designed and typeset in Palatino and Helvetica by
Meg Richardson (meg@pelinorepress.co.uk).

Printed in Great Britain by The Nuffield Press Ltd., Abingdon, Oxon.

A Handbook for

Deterring Plagiarism

in Higher Education

Second Edition

Jude Carroll

Oxford Centre for Staff and Learning Development

ASKe

ASKe (Assessment Standards Knowledge exchange), based in the Business School at Oxford Brookes University, is one of 74 Centres for Excellence in Teaching and Learning (CETLs) across the UK. It was set up in summer 2005 with a £4.5 million award from HEFCE in recognition of good practice based on pedagogic research into aspects of assessment.

One of ASKe's stated aims is to pioneer evidence-based practice by funding and supporting projects that seek out and cultivate ways to develop and enhance assessment practices. ASKe is therefore very pleased to sponsor this second edition of *A Handbook for Deterring Plagiarism in Higher Education*.

To find out more about ASKe and its work, please visit

www.business.brookes.ac.uk/aske.html.

Contents

Acknowledgements (second edition)

I reiterate the thanks I offered for the first edition. Although I can acknowledge published writers and speakers in the conventional way in my text, this is the only place where I can thank other key contributors. I am now grateful to thousands (rather than the original 'hundreds') who have helped me shape my ideas. My thanks go to colleagues, lecturers, students and participants at workshops – all have helped me hone and develop my thoughts. I appreciate their willingness to try out and evaluate new activities. I am indebted to those who tried out my ideas in their own institutions and offered feedback on their impact.

I also thank my critics who cite a statement I made in the acknowledgements of the first edition to the effect that I cannot always remember the origins of my own ideas about student plagiarism. This inability is even more pronounced now. The number of people who publish in the field of student plagiarism increased sharply around the time of the publication of the first edition and continues to grow. Discussions within institutions and indeed, nationally and internationally, are moving slowly towards consensus. All this activity means 'common knowledge' about the issue of student plagiarism and the ways we can address it is increasing. This consensus merits celebration. Critics' suggestion that I (and by implication all academics) ask of our students what we cannot deliver ourselves has encouraged me to become ever more explicit about what I understand by student plagiarism. I know now that this explicitness is a vital first requirement for encouraging students, colleagues and universities to be equally clear.

Finally, I thank my new colleagues in the Centre for Excellence, ASKe (Assessment Standards Knowledge exchange), who supported this second edition. Though the context has changed since 2002, I hope the second edition of the Handbook will continue to help those who are serious about addressing student plagiarism to decide where and how to start.

Acknowledgements (first edition)

Many people have directly and indirectly contributed to my ideas and understanding of plagiarism. Some of their contributions can be recognised in the conventional way by citation and bibliography and I have tried to do this in the text itself. Here, I can thank a few people directly and admit I can no longer remember exactly where an idea, insight or new activity came from. Many of the suggestions appear frequently in guides like this one – perhaps that makes them common knowledge? Many just seem like common sense but perhaps someone somewhere claimed this idea and I ought to cite it. I can no longer remember if the example of an essay that mentions the Princess of Wales as if she was alive (a trigger for further investigation of students copying previous work, surely) is one I thought up or one I encountered. In this matter, I resemble students who often feel a similar sense of confusion when knowledge now feels a part of oneself. I have learned from chats at conferences, corridor conversations with friends, or emails passing on student quotes like, 'I had a student this week who admitted the plagiarism but said he wasn't to blame because the person he copied from didn't tell him it was plagiarised….' If I have passed off someone else's work as my own in this Handbook, I apologise and would welcome this being drawn to my attention.

Some help is easy to acknowledge because it is still directly linked in my mind to the helper: Jon Appleton for sharing his skill at developing and clarifying policy matters and for the ideas in Chapter 8; Hazel Peperell who knows more about electronic detection than I ever will and who regularly demonstrates the capacity for creative detective work; Gill Chester who asked me to begin writing in this area as part of the JISC project and then became a generous networker; Paul Richardson, Margaret Price and Lynne Errey who commented on the text and suggested changes; Clare Collinson, Meg Richardson and Elizabeth Smith who turned a scruffy manuscript into a book; and my colleagues in the Oxford Centre for Staff and Learning Development who tolerated all the traumas of authorship.

Above all, I thank the hundreds of colleagues, lecturers, students and participants at workshops I have run over several years and in several countries. Their reactions and feedback have taught me what works for staff and students and what activities are important if we are serious about doing something about plagiarism.

Preface

Suggestions on using this book and a few words of advice

Often, people approach the issue of student plagiarism with a specific concern. For example, they might wish to revise their assessment, revamp the student induction programme or improve the consistency of how cases are managed. This Handbook is designed to address a specific aspect of deterring and dealing with student plagiarism in each chapter. Based on my experience of watching a large number of institutions tackle the issue, there does not seem to be one best place to begin – you can start anywhere. If you already know your reason for reading this book, you could start with the first chapter and then dip in and out of the others as and when they seem relevant. However, that same experience of watching people tackle the issue tells me that a local approach which addresses one aspect of the issue usually leads on to other actions rather than to a sense of satisfaction for a problem resolved.

Plagiarism is a complex issue. Whilst it is possible to use chapters in isolation and to start anywhere in your effort to deter student plagiarism, each action you take will rely on and be strengthened by actions taken to address other aspects. So, for example, thinking about induction relies on the subsequent attention to teaching the skills students need to avoid plagiarism. Reviewing penalties will also necessitate thinking about who delivers them. This type of interconnection is increasingly referred to in the plagiarism literature as 'holistic'. In a holistic approach, all aspects work together to deter students from submitting others' work as their own. A holistic approach also checks that students have complied with the regulations that require them to 'do their own work' and deals with those who do not in ways that are fair, defensible and consistent. This Handbook is strongly underpinned by a belief that the holistic approach is the only way to address the issue of student plagiarism.

The holistic approach is not easy but more and more institutions have shown it is possible, even given their constraints on time and resources. Many of the examples in the Handbook are drawn from a range of tertiary institutions in the UK and around the world where actions have started as small, local initiatives then grown to include the whole institution. Conversely, some are drawn from cases where top-down decisions on institutional change led to gradual changes in local practices and procedures. Both approaches have been effective.

If you are embarking on a more holistic approach, you will find suggestions in all the chapters that might prove helpful, though you probably need to do it all – eventually. Since this Handbook is designed to encourage action rather than be a literature review aimed at reflection, the following advice might be helpful, whichever approach you take:

Start small, start simply

It is possible to make a difference by adopting a single action (at least as a start). Teachers have found ways to tackle plagiarism without it overwhelming other important considerations or, as a senior colleague put it, 'without it being centre stage the whole time'. If you spend half an hour thinking about the assessment task, you might find a way to move students towards constructing their assignment and away from spending a few thought-free moments on Google. Here's an example: instead of asking for an essay on 'Smoking and public health', ask your students to 'Find four websites devoted to deterring smoking and rank their likely impact on a specific population or group. Justify the ranking with examples from the sites and reference to the literature'. In this case, you have encouraged them to 'do their own work' and more importantly, to thereby do their own learning. (It is a useful side effect that you have also increased your ability to spot copying.) Other small changes are also likely to make a difference. Perhaps a 20-minute exercise that asks students to read a one-page text with the four in-text citations removed and to argue with each other about where they must be replaced will teach more than the traditional 'lecture on plagiarism'. Or perhaps a 15-minute slot in the induction programme will send the message, 'Pay attention. UK university study is a new game played by new rules. You need to learn them.'

Be realistic

You will encounter many suggestions in this Handbook and elsewhere about dealing with student plagiarism that are irrelevant given your own circumstances and interests. For example, I suggest in workshops (and in Chapter 3) that you check whether the student who submitted the assignment actually did it by using a viva or observing some of the activity necessary to create the work. Those with classes of 250 throw their hands up and cry, 'Impossible'. If you have a similar reaction to this or any other suggestion, you could ignore it – there are probably many other ways you could have a similar or even larger deterrent effect. Or you could modify the idea to match your context – for example, deciding to viva a randomly selected 10% of the cohort, giving a workable 25.

You also need to be realistic about how much time you have available and how much of your time can be devoted to deterring plagiarism. Even straightforward actions need time to plan, carry through and evaluate. Having limited time can be positive. Time constraints have underpinned many of the changes to policies and procedures outlined in Chapters 7 and 8 about collecting evidence and 'proving' a case. These changes mean using far less time than was necessary under former arrangements with no threat to underpinning quality and defensibility. However, some aspects will always take time. An hour-long lecture, though possibly helpful, will not ensure students have the skills they need to avoid plagiarism. That requires practice, feedback, discussion and more practice – usually over many months and sometimes years. Institutional change is perhaps the most time-consuming aspect of all. Most institutions take at least five years to move from having no strategies for dealing with student plagiarism to feeling that they can explain and defend their policies and procedures and that they are confident that the procedures are working.

You cannot achieve the more complex, long-term actions necessary for a holistic approach alone but will need to involve colleagues, the management, or even outside experts. One of the purposes of this Handbook is to alert you to future actions that, whilst not addressed at the moment, might be adopted later.

Be flexible, stay ready to change your approach

As institutions get better at addressing their current worries, new ones will probably arise. Even while I was rewriting this edition, the literature on student plagiarism moved on, new ways popped up for students to post work for others to complete (so-called 'bidding sites') and the UK Office of Independent Adjudicators renewed their call for more consistent treatment. You are probably dealing with similar changes: increasing concerns about international students, perhaps, or debates about electronic ways to spot copying, or newspaper reports of the latest 'scandal'. Equally, you may find that what works with one group of students or one problem won't work with the next. All this means that this Handbook or your prior efforts will be overtaken by events and new technologies. Hopefully, the variety of ideas and suggestions under each of the headings in this Handbook will trigger your rethinking and review.

Check your own beliefs and motivation

I usually have no difficulty getting people to explain what worries them about student plagiarism. Nor is it hard to elicit explanations for not taking action to deal with it, either as an issue in itself, or as exemplified in a particular case. 'Blind eyes' are turned because people fear the time it takes to do something about an individual case. People tell me they worry that any action might be challenged by colleagues or senior managers, sometimes even to the point where they feel that they themselves, rather than their students, must explain themselves. Teachers worry that their relationship with students might be at risk, or that their sense of what is fair and justified might be compromised, given that their students often are unaware of what is expected or unprepared to deliver it. It seems fairly easy to get people to explain why they do not take action when they spot plagiarism and why they do not address the underpinning issues. I have never found that addressing these reasons directly leaves the other person reassured or minded to act. Instead, I offer this Handbook in the hope that anyone with a reason for not acting might discover for themselves a range of practical ways of doing the opposite – i.e. for taking action.

Institutions, colleagues and students must play their part if we are to halt or even reverse the growing number of students who try to gain credit for work they did not do. This is especially important if we are to catch and punish the small but growing number of students who seek academic credit by fraudulent means rather than through legitimate effort. Opportunities for deliberate cheating and for serious breaches of academic regulations seem to increase year on year. All students who submit others' work rather than making their own will bypass learning; some also exemplify behaviours and attitudes that are unacceptable. None have the graduate attributes we expect.

I think that regulations and, above all, that student learning are worth defending and I hope, once you have used this Handbook in whatever way seems best to you, that you will, too.

Reviewing the issues

Defining plagiarism?

> **Think about:**
>
> Are you, your colleagues and your students clear about the distinction between:
>
> - cheating and plagiarism?
>
> - copyright and plagiarism?
>
> - plagiarism and poor academic practice?
>
> - collaboration and collusion?

If a university policy has been revised in the last few years, it probably begins with a relatively simple statement in ordinary language as to what the word 'plagiarism' means. Often, this is followed by examples of unacceptable behaviours. Here is a typical example:

> Plagiarism is defined as submitting someone else's work as your own.

Whilst the statement seems straightforward, many studies have shown that students and staff understand it differently and many do not understand it at all. (See, for example, Freewood, 2001; Devlin, 2003; Shi, 2004). In fact, rather than the single question, 'What is plagiarism?', teachers, students, assessors, quality assurance professionals and managers need to develop shared answers to a range of questions such as:

- What do we in this department mean by the phrase 'submitting someone else's work as your own'?

- What constitutes plagiarism in an exam as opposed to coursework?

- What are our expectations for attribution in an oral presentation? In a group project?

- What do we consider to be plagiarism in our own discipline – i.e. in Graphic Design or History or Engineering?

- What are our expectations for first-year students – how well must they use citation conventions?

In my experience, nearly everyone has their own answers to such questions (or they do once someone prompts them to think about them). Through discussion, examples and even argument, consensus does develop. Students, in their turn, need to go through a very similar process to understand what is required by phrases such as 'do the assignment as an individual piece of work' or 'use your own words'. There are suggestions of how you might start this process with your own students in Chapter 4 on induction. The following paragraphs outline the tacit and implicit understanding that underpin definitions of plagiarism.

Assumptions underpinning plagiarism

One way to understand a statement such as 'submitting someone else's work as your own' is to examine the assumptions underpinning the words. 'Submitting' acknowledges the distinction between private and public work - it is only plagiarism when you 'go public', i.e. when a student hands in work. Since most coursework develops in stages with students encouraged to work together for some (or even all) of them, the definition on its own cannot cover collusion. Where do students stop co-operating and start to create work that, at submission, fails to make clear to the assessor whose work is being judged? There is more on this matter on pages 18 and 19.

'Submitting' is also a neutral term, describing an action without implying intent. Some definitions use terms that include intent such as 'passing off' – in this case, trying to trick someone, probably deliberately. Some definitions include value judgements or even emotive terms such as 'stealing' or 'cheating'. An example of this tone is the Student Guide for the UK Centre for Legal Education:

> Plagiarism is the word given to a particular kind of academic dishonesty – passing off someone else's work, ideas or words as your own. Plagiarism, whatever the source of the material or the intended outcome, is cheating and unacceptable. It is important to understand that intention does not have a role to play in the definition of plagiarism. Not meaning to do it, or not knowing you are doing it, is therefore not an excuse – and now that you have read this, you are aware of what it is.

Other policies have similar wording. Indeed, I used to advocate including the phrase 'intentionally or unintentionally' in a definition on

In my own subject area of dance... I can recall two instances when an investigation of plagiarism in student practical submissions has been necessary. On one occasion, an assessor viewed her own choreography... presented without acknowledgement. On another, assessors recognised material from a professional work...

Stevens (2002)

the grounds that students needed to know that an act could be plagiarism even if it arose from misunderstanding or poor compliance with referencing conventions. Now I think it is not helpful to conflate definitions with consequences or values although intent is highly relevant to determining what happens when a case is confirmed (see Chapter 7 for detailed discussion of this point). If you are devising a definition, this point about what to include or exclude will need careful thought.

'Work' is mentioned in the definition, not just others' words. Student plagiarism is different from other sorts of plagiarism in that it concerns itself with work that is submitted for academic credit. Students 'submit others' work' if they claim credit for others' efforts in, for example, finding information, organising it, thinking or drawing as well as if they submit others' writing. It is much easier to judge which aspects of work merit credit if the assessment criteria state this explicitly. For example, does the grade reflect the student's research efforts or just the way information was used?

The word 'work' was discussed in the previous paragraph as a verb (something that the student does to produce an assignment) but it is also a noun (the thing that is created). Concerns about plagiarism go beyond what is covered by copyright to include such things as constructions, images, compositions and ideas. Some definitions of plagiarism explicitly focus on how the submitted work is judged, defining plagiarism as '...creating a false assumption in an assessor by borrowing, without specific acknowledgement, from other published or unpublished work'. (Note: this definition also seems to narrow the definition of 'work' to words.)

Returning to the definition, the phrase 'someone else's work' implies a complex collection of assumptions and academic tradition. Many authors (for example Hunt, 2004; Levin, 2006) point to the inherent impossibility of individual ownership since all work is derived from and based on the ideas and efforts of others. Others (McGowan 2005; Pennycook, 1996; Handa and Power, 2005) stress that students' previous study may have included different assumptions about 'ownership' of ideas and about the value of attribution. Conventions for claiming work include publication, posting on the internet, saying things publicly in a conference, etc. As students become fully-fledged members of the academic community, they also need to pick up courtesies such as acknowledging things you have heard from others ('personal communication') or words and ideas that cropped up in informal discussions on the Web or face-to-face.

'Even if I do say so myself' may need to finish with a citation if you are quoting something that you have already published. Copyright to previously published work usually belongs to the publisher.

Evans (2000)

Conventions for signalling ownership such as in-text citation, quotation marks and stock phrases such as 'Brown states that....' can seem mysterious. Sometimes, students see them as just one more thing to organise. So, for example, as well as doing the work they must create logs of group activities, introductions that spell out who did what, colour coding sections of a group report to denote responsibility, etc. Students will need to see examples then try them out with feedback (probably several times) before they can navigate these issues confidently. (See Chapters 4 and 5 for suggestions on how to encourage this.)

The definition of plagiarism that refers to 'someone else's work' also incorporates the converse: that some work is common knowledge and/or cannot be attributed to any one person. Again, this idea turns out to be more than the question, 'What needs a reference?', though that question is hard enough for students new to the discipline or to the UK cultural context to answer. Students need to develop their own sense of when an attribution will strengthen and augment their argument; when a citation will allow the reader to check veracity; and when it will show the student to be someone who is 'out there' checking out sources, finding new material and evaluating its authority. In the meantime, students will welcome rule-of-thumb rules such as 'If it appears in two encyclopaedias it might be common knowledge…' and your tolerance if they over-cite whilst learning to find the right balance.

Finally, many definitions refer to submitting 'as your own [work]'. This is the bit of the definition that causes the most confusion. Students wonder, 'What turns work from being something that belongs to someone else into something that belongs to me?'. Sometimes, students resolve the issue by conforming to pragmatic rules ('never quote more than five words without using quote marks') or adopt surface strategies such as paraphrasing via a thesaurus ('instead of large, I'll write big'). Novice writers and those working in a second language often select and patch together a number of texts (with or without attribution) and view the result as a new and original text – and some would argue that indeed it is, calling this skill 'patchwriting'. I often meet students who devise their own meaning for the phrase 'my own work'. I remember one who insisted the work was her own because she had paid for the book from which she had copied.

What *does* make the work 'the student's own'?

The link between 'making your own work' and 'making your own learning' is what differentiates student plagiarism from plagiarism that happens outside higher education. Student plagiarism allows learners to bypass or avoid learning. This can happen deliberately through

A writing skills teacher explains:

Students often say they have been told to make a point and then 'find a quote to back it up'. They think it is the quotation itself that authorises or provides evidence for their point rather than the reference to a scholar's findings. They do not realise that they could summarise the findings and give the reference without the quotation. Thus, if they are told not to 'quote too much', some think they must avoid reference to the sources and are perplexed as to what they could find to say about a topic after six weeks of study…
This is sometimes the explanation for essays that veer off the topic or rely on the writer's opinions.

Chanock (2003)

misconduct. Students deliberately avoid learning if they pay someone to write coursework, or submit the same piece of work in two different courses, or copy large chunks of someone else's words or hand in someone else's solution. Students can inadvertently bypass learning through misunderstanding. For example, a student may think that the teacher is only interested in something being submitted ('He wanted some 3000 words and here are some I found'). Many students start their university study still assuming that copying the recognised answer from the textbook is what is required because it has always been acceptable in the past.

In reality, teachers are not just interested in coursework as 'stuff'. They must allocate credit for students' understanding as evidence that the student has met the learning outcomes. In the UK, students show understanding by changing or transforming others' ideas and words (and where they do not change them, they must quote them directly). A change that shows understanding could be a paraphrase of the previous text to fit the new circumstances (a very different thing from using the 'find and replace' function to change every fifth word). The change could be applying the ideas to a new context, or taking a theory to bits and looking at the component parts. Students transform knowledge when they answer questions 'in their own words' after an oral presentation because they construct the sentences, even if they do so using stock phrases or by importing words that others have also used. In all these examples, the student's work is 'original' in the sense of 'originating from the student'. Students and other writers (see, for example, Levin, 2004) can be deeply concerned about the notion of 'original' with some opting for meanings such as 'creating something novel' or 'something that previously did not exist'. This is not what is asked of undergraduates and usually characterises work at PhD and sometimes, master's level. (Students towards the end of undergraduate study come close in tasks such as honours dissertations where they are expected to collect data and make sense of it.)

Teachers will have their own ideas about how much change is necessary in order to demonstrate understanding and to meet the requirements that the work is the student's own. Whatever teachers' views, they need to be sure they are looking for evidence of students' learning rather than checking only for the finer points of referencing. Of course, students almost always need to know how to use a specific referencing system or where to put commas in a reference list – it's part of learning to be a student. Doing 'the referencing' correctly matters when a student publishes in a journal (though there will always be a copy-editor to help). It matters when students complete and publish a work such as a PhD dissertation or MA thesis. And it matters for high-status

[Student uncertainty] can create anxiety and fear of inadvertent plagiarism for some students. For example, it was felt by a number of first years that you could get accused and punished for plagiarising an idea they thought was their own but had in fact already been thought of and written in a book.

Freewood (2001, p. 2)

documents, such as honours theses, which showcase students' scholarship. In a much wider range of assessment tasks, students will need to be able to use citation convention to show how their ideas build upon and draw authority from the work of others. They will need to ensure the reader/marker knows where their ideas and others' ideas start and finish. None of this happens quickly so students will need to be introduced to citation conventions early, to be taught how they work, and receive feedback on their efforts.

Only over time will students come to see the activities described in the last paragraph as anything other than a nuisance or even stop seeing them, as Levin says, as akin to learning to 'dance with your shoelaces tied together' (Levin, P. quoted in Peverett, 2004). They will be helped to attend to these matters and will accept that the institution regards these behaviours as important aspects of academic integrity (as well as a way of showing courtesy) if they see the regulations being defended. Students who do not comply with these requirements (once alerted to their importance) need actions that show them that the breach matters. I often meet academics who overlook early breaches or deduct a few marks when students fail to cite. They add margin comments ('Where are your references?') or even do nothing on the grounds that 'the students are learning'. Though well intentioned, this approach is usually ineffective. A few students will take note. Most will continue to act as they did in previous academic/professional settings rather than attend to the new 'rules of the game'. Many students settle into strategies for finding or patching work together in their university assignments without realising that they risk harsh sanctions at a later stage in their academic life. (See Chapter 7 for a discussion of proportionate penalties that acknowledge students' apprenticeship.)

Defining collusion

'Collaboration' describes the work of learning and is highly valued by teachers and learners. As soon as a student submits work done jointly as if it had been done individually or passes off work where no student effort was involved, perhaps by copying, then he or she is giving a false impression to the assessor, either intentionally or unintentionally. This is collusion. Many students complain that the distinction between co-operation and collusion is not made clear and that they are not given guidance on how to show individual effort and learning. The distinction becomes especially problematic when a cohort is set a task with a single correct answer or resulting in a similar artefact. This issue is addressed in Chapter 2 on course design and in Chapter 4 on informing students. The exercise on page 19 is one way to start a discussion with your students as to your personal definition of collusion.

Collusion continuum

A teacher sets this task: 'Choose one of the three companies I suggest and write an individual report on their advertising campaigns in the last three years'.

Three students do the steps listed below in this order. When (if ever) do they move from co-operation and collaboration to creating a report that gives a false impression to the assessor as to whose work is being marked?

The three students:

1. Discuss the coursework brief with the teacher and with other students.

2. Look at examples of similar coursework from the past and discuss their good and bad points with each other.

3. Discuss the best way to tackle the task of writing the report and decide to all choose the same company ('Let's all do Microsoft').

4. Decide to all do a bit of research on advertising campaigns (*You find out about design, I'll do impact, Joe, you do cost, etc.*).

5. Tell each other what they found and brief each other on useful sources of information.

6. Photocopy each others' scribbles, library notes and printed Web pages.

7. Delegate the best researcher of the group to find out about the company's campaign, tell the others and give them copies of notes, Web pages, summaries of articles, etc. (*Joe, you find out and tell us...*).

8. Jointly agree a structure for the final report; agree which are the strongest points, which should go first etc.

9. Share out the writing task with each person writing one or two sections.

10. Pool the sections and everyone takes the collected text to write their own final draft. Nobody changes more than 5%.

11. Submit the report for a mark.

Defining plagiarism with students

Students usually find discussions of plagiarism either confusing or imminently ignorable. When they do delve deeper, students find them worrying – especially if they draw the conclusion that student writers must search high and low for prior claims for ideas they see themselves as generating. In reality, inadvertent overlooking of previous citations prompts feedback along the lines of 'check out X who has written widely about this'. I am not aware of a single case where a student has been accused of plagiarism because he or she overlooked a previously cited instance of something that the student claimed to have thought up. (If you, the reader, know of any such cases, I would welcome hearing about them.) But I have met masses of students who worry about this happening and I have read pages of text where the possibility is deplored as an affront to students' development as thinkers.

Why does plagiarism happen?

At one time, getting a top grade was not of compelling importance to many undergraduate students. The employment market and graduate careers were such that most students with lower-second degrees did not feel themselves to be seriously disadvantaged. Nowadays many students feel that anything less than an upper-second-class degree will irretrievably damage their career prospects. At the same time, many have less time to study because they are in effect 'working their way through college' or coping with heavy caring responsibilities.

McDowell and Brown (2001)

Some plagiarism statistics:

- Bull and Collins et al (2001) surveyed 321 UK academics and found that 70% believed that plagiarism was a 'significant problem in academic institutions' and 50% believed the problem had increased in recent years.

- An annual survey of American students (McCabe, 2005) found that in 1999, 13% said they regularly cut-and-pasted text into their papers without attribution. In 2002, 41% said they did so and in 2005, 38% said they copied without attribtuion. A similar question to UK students (Szabo and Underwood, 2004), found that 15% 'used the copy/paste function to embed material from the internet without modification and/or proper referencing into assignments' more than once a week; another 10% said they did so 'about once a week'. The authors concluded that for 6% of respondents, 'cheating appeared to be a way of life' (p. 190).

- In 2002, a study in Australia of 1,770 papers using a text-matching tool found that 8.8% of papers contained more than 25% of text that matched the text in their databases. A similar study of 30,000 papers in the UK in 2005 found that 13% of the papers had over 75% of the text matching that held in the databases. A study by Culwin (2006) reported on four years' tracking of students in a first-year computing programme using a tool he designed with colleagues. He concluded that behaviours varied widely. 'About 20% of the students submitted work that was more than 50% non-original. At the same time, about 50% of the students submitted work that was shown to contain less than 20% non-original work.'

- In 2006, Lambert et al surveyed NZ students in two tertiary institutions. 70% said they knew of occurrences where someone paid another person to do an assignment; 78% knew of cases where one person had written an assignment for someone else; 49% had experience of someone copying at least once from someone without their knowledge; and 91% had falsified data from their research. The authors included comments from students such as: 'Everyone cheats, especially in exams.' 'It happens, you don't get through without cheating.' 'Everyone cheats at some time or other, especially on assignments. I think lecturers realise this' and 'Plagiarism is riff' [sic].

- In 2006, one site (ukessays.com) said they had supplied 15,000 people with 'tailor-made essays' since the business began in 2003. In one week in May 2006, the owner said students had purchased £90,000 worth of 'research' in the form of 'model essays'. The journalist who wrote the story estimated the UK market was worth £200m per year (*The Guardian*, 29 July 2006).

Students studying at postgraduate level and/or those experienced in higher education assignments generally welcome discussions that make the ideas underpinning definitions of plagiarism transparent. Novices often value more concrete requirements while they are finding their feet. So, with first-year students, you might talk about why 'your own work' matters but suggest that as a rule-of-thumb, if a student uses more than five (eight, ten, twelve…whatever seems appropriate) words, then it would be wise to use quotation marks. Many of the activities in Chapter 5 will also be useful. Whenever you bring the issue of plagiarism up, that is also a perfect lead into discussing why citing others will strengthen their writing and result in better marks.

How widespread is plagiarism?

> **Think about:**
>
> - what is your experience with student plagiarism?
>
> - what have you encountered or heard colleagues talking about?
>
> - what about your own student days? Did you cut corners, take shortcuts, make up citations or collude with fellow students?
>
> - how seriously do you view the problem?

In 1995, the first major review of undergraduate cheating in the UK was published (Franklyn-Stokes and Newstead, 1995) with the useful subtitle 'who does what and why?' It opened the discussion of cheating in the UK and built on a large body of literature from the USA. The authors concluded that the British experience in the mid-1990s was similar to that reported in other countries, with more than 60% of students reporting 'behaviours such as copying each others' work, plagiarism and altering and inventing research data' (p. 159). Subsequent reports, studies and news articles, both in the UK and around the world, confirm a growing interest in and concern about plagiarism. However, rates and types of cheating and plagiarism have changed in the intervening decade. Indeed, some authors claim that any statistics quoted from before 1998, when the use of meta-search engines became widespread, and any that pre-date the relatively widespread use of text-matching software are no longer relevant.

Assertions by academics and published statistics are tricky to evaluate. Most studies do not provide the context for their statistics and sometimes offer just a percentage. When you read '80% of students admit plagiarism' (Maslen, 2003), are they admitting to:

- a one-off event or serial plagiarism?

- copying a few lines of text or a significant portion of a work?

- cheating in a relatively minor piece of work or in one that will determine a degree classification such as a dissertation?

In fact, it is not necessary to determine exactly how big a problem plagiarism is to consider it to be a problem worth tackling. By its nature, plagiarism threatens the value and integrity of what is being taught. It threatens students' engagement with learning and, unless addressed, could undermine the worth of the awards students earn and the

We have introduced Turnitin here and I think - I'm not sure - that my students have started going back to the Library and reading books. It's too early to tell or to show a causal connection but I plan to watch and see.

One UK academic

reputation of UK higher education. Most people surveying the scene would agree with Park (2003) who concluded his extensive review of students' experiences with plagiarism by stating that plagiarism was 'doubtless common and getting more so' (p. 271).

Is it the Web?

The internet has changed students' behaviour. A study in 2001 (JISC, 2001) found that students were more likely to copy from text-based sources and some academics continue to say this is true, mentioning books, lecture notes and pre-memorised examination questions. I often hear lecturers in subjects such as Nursing or Early Childhood Studies say that they mark handwritten scripts and that their students rarely venture far from set texts without strong prompting. However, in most subjects, the balance has tipped towards digital copying ('cut-and-paste') and the statistics already cited confirm the trend. Concern about digital copying is high where students have access to a huge range of relevant resources (e.g. Business and Media Studies). They are high where teachers are likely to be less familiar with opportunities than their students (e.g. courses taught in English in non-English speaking countries) or where students' skills and inclinations tend towards the digital (e.g. Computing or Graphic Design). Some subjects such as Law are especially well provided with bespoke services and model answers. Some such as Mathematics, Accounting and Computing set tasks which lend themselves to seeking external help. One new way to do so is via so-called 'bidding sites' where students post coursework and accept an offer to complete it for a stated amount. All these opportunities are facilitated by the Web and addressing them requires a rethink of how assessment tasks are set and managed (see Chapters 2 and 3), since they are difficult to detect using standard approaches.

It is not hard to see why the Web has changed how students go about 'finding stuff'. Of course, such 'research' has its weaknesses: Google reaches only a percentage of the Web and only a small percentage of what it finds is derived from academic journals or reviewed publications. And it has risks. Mirow and Shore (1997) argue that digitalising text per se changes the relationship between author and reader and makes plagiarism more likely. They cite the invention of moveable type as a prompt to authors to regard their work as valuable and therefore worth defending from the wider readership's use. This, in turn, triggers copyright laws. Digitalising text means anyone can use it, manipulate it and seem to 'own' it and students become 'word brokers'. Once students detach blocks of texts from their original authors (often losing the attribution information through 'inattentive research practices' (p. 42)), they then treat the captured blocks as their own.

Oxbridge Essays

Oxbridge Essays provides individually written essays by graduates of Oxford and Cambridge... The company offers a next day delivery service at extra cost. A 2,000 word undergraduate essay of upper-second quality delivered in six days would cost £600 and a full undergraduate dissertation costs up to £5,400 depending on length and quality. [The Founder] emphasises the essays are intended as model answers and were not meant to be handed in as the student's own work but also notes 'Of course, most professors at British universities have large classes and are far too busy to ever check whether your essay has been written by you or not. They may even be too swamped to check whether the style of a given essay is really your own.'

Oxford Times,
14 April 2006

Students' understanding of acceptable ways to use Web-based information has not kept pace with its exponential growth. Gajadhar (1998) describes students' commonly-held belief that material on the Web is free for anyone to use, and/or the view that changing a few words makes a downloaded text 'my own work'. When Gajadhar asked students to classify scenarios involving the Web as either plagiarism or acceptable, their responses divided almost exactly 50/50, demonstrating student confusion.

It is less clear whether the Web has had an impact on students' decisions about how they generate their work. It does offer much greater opportunities, but other factors will also influence a student's decision on how they generate their work. More of these factors are reviewed on page 26.

Is the problem essay banks? Ghost writing services?

A growing number of so-called 'paper mills' offer essays for sale and student newspapers regularly alert students to their existence, though any student can easily locate one with a key word search of 'essay' plus the name of their discipline. Academics who visit the sites are often startled to find essays and research papers, both for sale and for free, catalogued by topic, level and discipline. There are sites offering outlines, 'study help' to edit your own paper for a guaranteed good grade, and guidance on how best to modify and adapt essays to get a good grade or to escape detection. For example, Markmyessays.com promises, 'We can help you and we guarantee a better mark!'

All these 'services' used to be regarded as an American phenomenon but are now widespread in the UK and becoming more common around the world. One UK-based site (www.academicdb.com) started in 2003 and by September 2006 offered 16,146 essays from GCSE to undergraduate level on the basis that students upload three and then have access to the database without paying a fee. This site and dozens of similar ones demonstrate both how the sector has grown and the fact that students can acquire the 'buy one' habit early in their academic life.

An enterprising approach

―――――――――

From 'a retired lecturer selling essays to students over the Internet': 'I would be very happy to write a series of essays for you, and complete the final year of your degree...You need not worry that the authorities would discover the work Is not your own. In some cases I can, if felt necessary [sic] that the work I am writing might seem as above the grade that could be attained by the student, actually build in material which I know is incorrect, so that the grade does not cause any alarm ... In any case, there has never been a student who has been subjected to a viva due to concern regarding the source or indeed questioned...'

―――――――――

Extract from an article by L. Major in The Guardian, *8 January 2002, p. 9*

Mixed messages

'Mary' is paid to write essays. She is quoted as saying, 'I'm proud of what I do. If I have helped someone who's been sweating it out and point them in the right direction, that gives me a sense of satisfaction'.

'Mary' refuses to give her own name.

'Mary' says she works full time as a 'legal executive' and also earns between £400 and £1,000 per week from commissioned essays. The company (ukessays.com) says it charges £240 for 2,000 words and keeps 30% so 'Mary' must write between 5,700 and 14,300 words per week.

The article does not say how long this writing takes 'Mary' or how she manages to meet such a demanding workload.

(*The Guardian*, 29 July, 2006 in an article by Mathew Taylor and Riazzat Butt under the headline:
Q: How do you make £1.6m a year and drive a Ferrari?
A: Sell essays for £400.)

There is no clear evidence as to how many commissioned or purchased essays are submitted for academic credit. Claims from site providers are hard to verify and open to commercial exaggeration. Did ukessays.com actually receive 60 or 70 requests per day from one university town for bespoke essays as they claim happened in June 2006? Does one provider actually sell 1,000 essays a week as she said at a 2004 plagiarism conference? Small-scale surveys show their impact is tiny or nonexistent (FreshMinds, 2004), yet many students say they know people who use such 'services'. My children tell me they have been asked to write for pay by fellow students. An increasing number of academic staff say they provide the material. All this anecdotal evidence suggests the issue cannot be ignored and most institutions are considering how to manage its impact. This usually means a combination of the suggestions in Chapters 2 and 3 to encourage students to make rather than fake their assignments as well as more effective use of detection strategies as outlined in Chapter 6. Many studies have shown that students who take this route of deliberate misconduct do so after calculating the risk of being caught and the consequences should this happen (Bennett, 2005; Burkhill and Franklyn-Stokes, 2004; Freewood, 2001).

Have you been slacking off all year? Need a dissy fast and can't be arsed doin it?

Fully completed 6000 word dissy with reference list under the topic 'Gender differences in anxiety in sport' covers all background research on anxiety, very useful!!!!!! The dissertation was given a 2nd class mark, excellent if you have missed lectures all year and your tutor won't believe you if you hand in a 1st class paper purchased on the internet! Genuine mistakes included, along with graphs, tables and all the files needed for a complete dissy. All in Microsoft word, just hand it in as it is, or modify to suit, you decide.
Ultimate Lazy Persons Solution
Wish I had bought one instead of actually doing it!

Verbatim extract from Ebay, accessed November 2004

Reasons students give (not in order of frequency)	What might lie behind the statement
I got desperate at the last moment	poor personal time management; juggling multiple demands
I could not keep up with the work	poor personal time management; bunched assessments; multiple deadlines; poor information provided about deadlines
The tutor doesn't care so why should I?	perceived disinterest in the course content, in the student or in the student's learning; no enthusiasm shown by teacher; tutor using outdated or unchanged materials
I have to succeed – everyone expects me to succeed and I expect it too	parental pressure; cultural expectations; costs of the course; living expenses; not being in employment, etc.
I don't understand what I'm expected to do to avoid plagiarism	unclear definitions; unclear instructions on referencing; lack of experience in (UK) academic writing
I can't do this! I'll have to copy	assignments perceived as beyond the student's ability; unclear assignment specifications; procrastination
I want to see if I can get away with it / I'll probably get away with it	testing the system; challenging authority; perceiving relatively minor penalties (or, if the 'penalty' is resubmission, a benefit!) as worth the risk
I don't need to learn this, I just need to pass it	prerequisites and mandatory courses that provide no intrinsic motivation with exclusively extrinsic goals, e.g. a students' award, certification
But you said, 'work together'!	misunderstanding of the role of collaboration in learning; misunderstanding of the need to submit individualised work for assessment; lack of shared understanding of what constitutes 'collusion'
But paraphrasing would be disrespectful/dangerous/nonsense	assumptions about how one treats experts' ideas; a lack of confidence in paraphrasing skills, especially in a second language

I often hear students say 'I deserve a 2.1.' They seem to regard work as currency and they are trading their time for a guaranteed result.

A university teacher

The reasons given for plagiarism in the table above are based on material in 'Plagiarism Detection and Prevention, the final report on the JISC electronic plagiarism detection project' (Chester, 2001).

Students' decision-making

> ### Think about:
>
> - why do your students plagiarise?
>
> - do you believe their explanations?
>
> - how frequent is it?
>
> - how might you find out?

Some academics dispute the relevance of studies on student motivation saying, 'I don't care why they do it, I just tell them it's not allowed and there are penalties for those who don't obey the rules.' As the definition of plagiarism cited on page 13 acknowledges, plagiarism is plagiarism, whether or not it is intended. On the other hand, Bannister and Ashworth (1998) claim that unless we understand 'the place and possible meanings of cheating within the student lifeworld' (p. 233), then any attempts to understand the statistics and tackle the issue will be misguided.

Reasons and explanations for plagiarism vary. Cox et al (2001) asked staff and students why plagiarism occurs and found that two-thirds of the respondents cited students' poor time management as the most common cause, with staff citing this much more frequently than students. The authors add that 'needing more help [was] also a popular choice'. Cox found that it was only undergraduates who cited the work being 'too hard' as a reason for cheating. Those who took this view constituted only a third of all respondents. The same study found that postgraduates and staff were much more likely than undergraduates to attribute cheating to poor supervision, to work not being checked, and/or to a low risk of being caught (but the frequency remained low at about 30% of the total). In general, academics offer both students' poor personal organisation and their lack of understanding as equally likely to underpin cheating behaviour.

Bennett (2005) took a different approach and looked for factors associated with students' self-declared plagiarism. He differentiated between minor plagiarism (copying 'a couple of sentences', citing fictitious references, collaborating with a friend on work that should have been completed individually) and major plagiarism (copying 'a number of paragraphs' or 'an entire piece of work'). For minor plagiarism, he found the strongest links were with students' attitudes towards the practice as fundamentally improper, and with 'the degree of an individual's academic integration. Students whose part-time employment interfered with their studies; who were obtaining low

Lack of rhetorical confidence can easily lead to patching, when in fact the student has good content understanding. Such cases might need augmented modes of assessment such as a brief interview. Even the shift from 'plagiaphrasing' (unacceptable) to 'conventional academic writing' is not always clear, even to academics.

Biggs (1999, p. 130)

27

When I get nervous about writing up my thoughts in poor English even when I know the subject OK, I can't think. So I use other people's words.

Student in the Errey study (Errey, 2001)

grades and/or were under heavy parental pressure to succeed were more likely to plagiarise' (p. 152). Major plagiarism, on the other hand, was most closely linked to three variables: fear of failure encouraged major plagiarism; fear of the penalties discouraged it; and the relationship with the teacher had an impact. On the last point, Bennett reports one 'unanticipated' finding: '[s]tudents who reported they had an excellent relationship with their lecturers confessed to engaging in major plagiarism to a substantially greater extent than others' (p. 152). He postulates that these students either thought the breach would be overlooked or would not result in severe penalties if detected.

For some students, such as international students, these complexities are an everyday challenge. Students say they ask themselves a number of questions before tackling assignments: Where should I put my energy: should it go into finding the answer that someone else has made or into making an answer myself? How likely is it that I will do a 'good' one or even a 'good enough' one? If I don't do this task, what else will suffer? If I do do the task, what else will suffer? Is the task worth doing? How likely is it that I will be caught if I plagiarise? Are the penalties if I am caught severe enough to cause me concern? Chapters 2 and 3 suggest how these questions can guide decision on programme and task design.

International students' motives

Think about:

* are international students a special case?

* do they have different motivations from home students?

* how might you explain the higher rates of plagiarism in international students that are commonly reported in UK higher education?

I know what plagiarism is. We have it in Korea too, and we take it very seriously. I do not cheat deliberately. But I get into trouble when I write because I know some subject knowledge better than other and I can write it better. So the lecturer thinks I am cheating when it is my knowledge and I write it better than other times.

Student in the Errey study (Errey, 2001)

There is a growing literature on the issue of how international students deal with plagiarism. Explanations vary as to why the number of cases that involve international students, as a percentage of the total, usually exceeds and sometimes far exceeds the percentage of international students in the cohort. Some see the over-representation of international students in punishment statistics as an artefact of detection. They point out that since most academics use change of language as the most significant clue to spotting a student who is copying someone else's words and some use only this clue (Bull et al, 2001), then that change of language is much easier to spot in a non-native writer.

It is also common to hear international students' apparent tendency to plagiarism linked to differences in academic cultures. I regularly meet academics who say their students believe that verbatim copying signifies respect for authority and some add that international students come from cultures where knowledge is held communally, available to all, and their students continue to hold that view. Is this correct? It is true that many international students come from systems where memorising and reproducing information is highly valued (as, indeed, do many A-level students). Many come from countries where adherence to international conventions on copyright may be inactive or under-stressed. (Note: All countries with the exception of North Korea and Mayanmar have agreements to comply with the Berne conventions on copyright that underpin whatever local variations exist in particular states and territories.) Many students also assume that the norms or rules from previous study settings should still apply. For example, Walker (1998) describes a study of postgraduates who 'made little attempt to conceal their [collusion] and argued that since their own cultural norms not only tolerated such behaviour but actually required it in the tradition of assisting a friend in need, it should likewise be tolerated by the … school' (p. 93).

Not everyone accepts that the best way to explain apparently high levels of plagiarism is through reference to cultural beliefs. I have academics tell me that their students cite culture because it is less stigmatising than lack of ability. Errey (2001) interviewed 46 students from a wide range of countries in their third term of study in a UK university (undergraduate and postgraduate) and 30 academic staff who taught them. Most of the academics cited cultural difference as the reason for students not complying with British conventions but none of the students did so. All the students knew that British universities would punish them if they plagiarised and most said they had similar rules in their home countries. Graham and Leung (2004) reported a study in Hong Kong where a clear majority stated that copying others' work was 'not good' or 'not acceptable' but only a small minority wanted it treated harshly as they empathised with fellow students who found work too hard, fell behind, and/or found the tasks meaningless. Shi (2004), in an interesting study that compared how Canadian and Chinese students tackled the same writing task, found that both groups knew they must change the text and cite the original author(s) but the Canadians did so explicitly, citing the author as a named individual, whereas the Chinese students 'tuck[ed] away the author in a less central position' (p. 184) and assumed the reader would know they were alluding to others' ideas.

While marking MA dissertations this summer, I noticed that my international students' writing was more stylistically appropriate and linguistically accurate in the literature review section than in the results or discussion sections. Looking at the work more carefully, I realized that the students had used the language from the literature review texts as a scaffold and this resulted in more academic sounding prose. When they wrote up, analyzed and discussed their results they had no scaffold so there were more instances of awkward phrasing and grammatical inaccuracy.

Schmitt (2005)

Schmitt (2005) links the high number of cases amongst international students with language competence:

> A lack of their own words to express their ideas is the most common reason students give for their reliance on the language of their texts in their writing. Therefore, while purchasing papers over the internet or copying with the intent to deceive is clearly plagiarism, it is less clear that borrowing the words of others in an attempt to find one's own voice in a new language should implicate one in a criminal act (p. 67).

She then goes on to explore how students acquire the language, ideas and underpinning cultural knowledge they need to become confident writers. Until they became so, downloading text often seems the best approach for all students. Many say this is especially true for international students, given their overwhelming need to succeed coupled with problems with meeting deadlines often arising from the work taking much longer than would be the case for UK students. Many non-native speakers avoid rewriting sources 'in their own words' even when they know this is expected, using a verbatim quote instead, for fear of losing the meaning through unskilful paraphrasing. Others say they lift and copy text because they find it hard to believe that the university wishes someone with imperfect English to rewrite the flowing prose of a native speaker (Angelil-Carter et al, 1999).

Whatever the explanation (and it is likely that most students' actions result from a combination), there is enough concern about international students as a specific group to warrant targeting extra resources and attention towards helping them develop acceptable and efficient reading and writing skills early in their UK academic life.

Real fear or media hype?

Press interest, startling headlines and discussions amongst worried academics often makes it seem as if plagiarism constitutes a systematic and wholesale assault on the assessment system in HE. A search using the word 'plagiarism' in the index of the UK *Times Higher Education Supplement* for 2005 returns 70 stories and another 54 in the first six months of 2006. In popular newspapers, the story is equally omnipresent under headlines that often preach panic and use metaphors of war (*'Defeat student cheaters'*, *'QAA to crack down on cheats'*), crime (*'Fingers in the word-till'*, *'The internet: a powerful tool for plagiarism sleuths'*) and disease (*'the plagiarism plague'*, *'the origins and ravages of plagiarism'*). In many cases, the story and the headline are ill-matched. For example, a 2005 report on Scottish examinations at the end of secondary school involving 140,000 candidates sitting 575

An overseas student said to me recently '...I copied the material straight from the Web because my English is not very good, and I wanted to make sure you understood what I was trying to say.'

Lecturer in HE

30

examinations said that 41 were reported for plagiarism and 11 of the cases were upheld. The text makes clear that ten times as many were penalised for using mobile phones yet the headline was 'Exam agency probes Web cheating'. (Over-selling the significance of this tiny percentage misses what I would consider a real story about under-detection.) The same exaggeration was evident when a Senior Proctor at Oxford University reported 10 cases in the 2004/5 academic year from over 17,000 students. The Proctor wrote, 'Plagiarism is becoming a serious problem' and later denied in interviews that the problem was rife (Grafen, 2006, p. 16). The story generated many headlines in national papers along the lines of 'Plagiarism rife at Oxford?' (see, for example, the *Daily Telegraph*, 14 March 2006).

This level of interest risks undermining confidence that the system is accrediting student effort – yet most students do not plagiarise. Many academic colleagues have told me they are reluctant to speak about their efforts to deal with plagiarism lest they find themselves in the national news. This is not an idle fear. In 2005, using information gathered via the Freedom of Information Act, a ranked list of UK universities by number of cases managed was created. The 'top' university managers found themselves on BBC national news answering questions about whether their degrees had credibility. In fact, their appearance on the list was more likely to be evidence of them taking the issue seriously. Named institutions had developed systems for managing large numbers of cases quickly so that staff now felt confident to report cases. Yet the *Daily Mail* extrapolated from the figures and issued stories about '20,000 cases of cheating' rather than the more likely story that institutions now viewed finding no cases as a threat to their reputation for quality assurance. (Nor did the '20,000 cases' headline remind readers that this represents a fraction of 1% of coursework in the HE sector.)

Students, too, might be affected by the growing concern and by the media's and external quality assurance bodies' repeated stress on preventing and catching cheaters. It could be that students who do not cheat - apparently the large majority - feel it is becoming harder to continue not to do so. One important way to reassure those adhering to regulations and to deter those considering breaking them is to encourage informed discussion with informed teachers about what the real worries might be.

I was on the inter-site bus recently and overheard two students exchanging information on who to use locally to write coursework. They had detailed and up-to-date information on the going rates (£10 an hour, apparently) and who was best for what kind of work. I didn't intervene - they weren't in my school - but I did go back and suggest to my course team that we convene a meeting to talk about it.

A UK academic

31

Reasons to be cheerful

Tackling plagiarism can mean adopting a range of approaches that are relatively straightforward and that are compatible with concerns about time and resources. Any institution or any individual interested in deterring, detecting and dealing with plagiarism can now draw on others' experience in doing so. Consensus about what constitutes good practice is emerging as is the growing willingness between institutions to discuss and share practices (even if journalists are less likely to report the trend). A small study I did with a colleague in 2005 confirmed that changes were underway and some evaluation of their impact is showing they are effective (Carroll and Duggan, 2005). This is encouraging. Some institutions around the world are being recognised for taking a measured, systematic and scholarly approach to dealing with the issue. The literature grows weekly. Suggestions and recommendations derived from others' experience and the literature are cited in subsequent chapters of this handbook. Best of all, changes designed to lessen plagiarism probably increase the amount of effort and learning you can encourage from your students. Potentially, this is a win-win situation all around.

Designing courses for deterring plagiarism

Some teachers advocate detection as the primary means for deterring plagiarism and research does suggest that students, too, see fear of being caught as 'one of the greatest deterrents' (Freewood, 2001). However, most teachers, even the most assiduous in checking for cheating, also see the benefit in changing their programmes and courses to make plagiarism less likely. This chapter suggests what you might design **in** to increase your students' chances of avoiding plagiarism, and how you might design **out** opportunities for easy plagiarism. But first, a word of warning: making any change on its own is unlikely to solve the problem of plagiarism. Only by adopting several suggestions, letting each strengthen and underpin the others and creating a sort of net of deterrence, will you make it more likely that students are learning, being assessed on their learning and avoiding shortcuts that bypass learning. Chapter 3 deals with specific aspects of assessment that could lessen plagiarism. Chapter 5 considers the teaching of skills that enable students to comply with academic conventions and do what a course asks of them.

> **Think about:**
> - what do you already know needs changing in the courses you lead?
> - if you are redesigning a course soon, who do you need to work with?
> - if you have collaborators, are they aware of the need to consider plagiarism?

Redesigning existing courses

Research on plagiarism supports the view that students are increasingly able to cheat, increasingly likely to submit work that is not their own, and increasingly unable to comply with academic rules and conventions (see Chapter 1). If your course was designed at a time when all these factors were easy to ignore, it would probably benefit from an audit now, so that specific ways to dissuade or deter plagiarism can be found.

An exercise in designing in and designing out opportunities for plagiarism

Building Bridges in Hot Countries

Learning outcomes for the course

As a result of this course, students will be able to:

1. describe how to build long and short bridges;

2. list factors affecting bridge construction in hot climates; and

3. solve problems in building construction in hot countries.

Assessment:

- A 2,000 word essay on the last day of the course on one of the following topics or one chosen by the student (40% of the final mark):

  1. Bridges in Ecuador;
  2. A history of bridge building in Nigeria; or
  3. How to build a bridge when the river floods a lot.

- A group project (45% of the final mark): the project will require a group of up to six students to produce a model of a bridge that would be capable of spanning a 50-ft chasm. The model must be able to fit on a phone book and must be made with the materials provided, i.e. matchsticks, string and card. Each group will be issued with the same materials. All members of the group will receive the same mark. All marks are awarded to the final product.

- Four case study reports of 500 words each (15% of the final mark): students will write up the weekly tutorial discussion of case studies after the session, submitting them the next week.

Some information about the course:

The course has run for the last five years in this format. Student projects are handed back at the end of term. Essays are not returned after marking. Case study material took considerable energy to develop because it uses examples that the lecturer experienced; they have not changed during the life of the course.

Plagiarism opportunity

a student could plagiarise any one of the assessments and not be any worse off for the rest.

Solution 1: integrate the tasks, perhaps substituting a computer simulation for the model and asking for a technical report that evaluates how successfully the simulated bridge was built; find a way to ensure that doing one task is necessary for doing the next.

Solution 2: test knowledge and skills – case studies could teach students to analyse situations and learn how to justify choosing certain actions; you could then test this learning in an unseen case study under exam conditions.

Collusion opportunity

all work is done out of sight.

Solution 1: observe some work, perhaps instead of some of the lectures.

Solution 2: require recording of activity and check it at specified times – logs, video diaries, threaded electronic discussions or project notes have been used (note: 'checking' does not mean assessing); peer checking might be possible and offers benefits, see page 44.

Plagiarism opportunity

the information requested is probably available on the Web or in a textbook in fully usable form.

Solution 1: work with this, asking students to demonstrate learning outcomes that value and require information gathering.

Solution 2: set tasks that ask students to find, compare and evaluate sites rather than simply plundering them.

Plagiarism opportunity

students could find one first, then 'choose' or choose a topic that suits a ghost writer's skills and knowledge.

Solution: don't allow last-minute changes.

Collusion opportunity

the whole group gets the same mark, regardless of individual contribution.

Solution 1: use the group task for learning but ask each person to submit something individually for assessment.

Solution 2: allocate some of the marks for peer assessment.

Solution 3: assess the process of building the model as well as the product itself.

Plagiarism opportunity

students could submit essays, case studies and models from previous years.

Solution: set new assessment tasks each time.

Plagiarism opportunity

students could find essays or information on the Web.

Solution 1: essays are easily available – ask instead for technical reports or case studies from your own situation or data.

Solution 2: use evaluative or analytical essay topics.

Solution 3: set specific, recent or narrow topics; specify requirements such as which sources to include.

Plagiarism opportunity

essays are only seen at submission allowing last-minute downloading, copying or purchase.

Solution: ask for a plan, drafts or outlines – do not mark them but sign and date them to verify they exist.

Plagiarism opportunity

anyone could have done the work that a student submits for assessment.

Solution 1: use vivas, in-class tests or oral presentations.

Solution 2: use observed meta-essays (see page 48).

New courses also need this kind of inspection. In either case, you might be too closely involved with the course to be able to detect opportunities for plagiarism. You may also be put off by worries about the time involved, and those new to course design may not be sure where to start.

One way to overcome reluctance to start reviewing your course is by considering a hypothetical example such as the one on page 34; you could also use this activity as a warm-up exercise if you share the redesign with a team of people. This course is called 'Building Bridges in Hot Countries'. Opportunities for plagiarism and collusion have been identified and possible solutions suggested.

Examples of designing out opportunities for plagiarism

Students are far less able to gain credit for work that is not their own (i.e. to plagiarise) in courses where there are:

- no chances to pass the course by submitting something that already exists;

- no chances to use others' work as evidence for assessment; and

- no processes for choosing and agreeing assessment tasks that might make fraud easy.

Examples of designing in aspects that will lessen plagiarism

Students plagiarise less on courses that include:

- links between assessment tasks so each builds on and confirms the rest;

- methods to track, observe and record student effort;

- acknowledgement of online information and encouragement to use online resources;

- ways for students to show individual effort and to create individual assessment artefacts;

- authentication exercises to ensure the student who gained the credit actually did the work; and

- opportunities for students to practise using academic writing skills, receive feedback and improve their practice.

I remember going into a lecture last year to observe and the handout still referred to xxx Polytechnic. I was embarrassed and the students just sniggered.

A lecturer in 2002

Suggestions for course design

Change the course requirements

This is perhaps the most straightforward place to start when considering how to lessen opportunities for plagiarism. Where essays have stayed the same year after year, the same case studies are issued (or only changed cosmetically by altering names or numbers), or when students are asked for tried-and-tested practicals, they are more likely to plagiarise. Franklyn-Stokes and Newstead (1995) confirm that students regard copying in such courses as simply common sense. Why should they make an effort when the lecturer does not?

Consider the learning outcomes

> **Think about:**
>
> * which are you asking students to do: to show they know or to use what they know?

Learning outcomes describe what students do to demonstrate their learning and the context within which their learning will be shown. Over the years, academics have developed a hierarchy of cognitive learning outcomes based on their complexity and derived from Bloom's taxonomy, named after one of its creators. Bloom's taxonomy describes how students learn by referring to different kinds of cognition. Each new level depends upon and therefore includes the previous ones, so assessing the higher levels (4, 5 and 6 below) will also check knowledge and comprehension.

Bloom's cognitive taxonomy:

1. Knowledge

2. Comprehension

3. Application

4. Analysis

5. Synthesis

6. Evaluation

Bloom's taxonomy is important when redrafting courses to lessen plagiarism because the lower levels (1 and 2: knowledge and comprehension), are much more likely to already exist. Asking students to 'show they know' can easily be interpreted as 'show you can find'.

Problem based learning will not always produce active, investigating students. One study of medical students found that they didn't start by investigating their learning needs: they commonly started by 'obtaining last year's objectives'. The study also showed that students did not see this 'undermining of the PBL ethics' as serious cheating.

Cogdell et al (2002) 'Academic cheating: an investigation of medical students' views of cheating on a problem-based learning course', Improving Student Learning, 10.

Asking a student to explain, list or collect information is seen by some as an invitation to recycle someone else's solution. On the other hand, asking students to demonstrate learning outcomes that provide evidence of more complex thinking greatly lessens the chances that they will copy or purchase a document that already exists. Students will need to make an effort to show they can use information in a specified context or even evaluate someone else's use of it, perhaps provided in a case study. The more analytical, specific and creative the task, the less likely the solution already exists and therefore, for the student, the task becomes 'create the solution' not 'find the solution'.

As well as changing learning outcomes, you could add one for information-gathering *per se*, including text and digital resources. Macdonald (2000) argues that collecting and using information is much closer to the employment experience of graduates than many others stressed in HE so it may also offer vocational value as well as encourage individual learning.

Create individualised tasks that result in individualised answers

Some courses set the same task for all students. Sometimes, this seems unavoidable because the skill is relatively straightforward, such as using an IT package or solving a practical problem. However, assessing application or comparison rather than use will encourage more individualised products. For example, instead of asking a question about patient care in general which might simply require all students to repeat back your lecture notes, ask students to identify a particular patient and consider how the general theory is relevant to that case.

The student's own experience

A Canadian lecturer, considering how best to deter plagiarism suggested setting assignments that 'use a personally relevant reference point such as the student's own home in architecture, own teeth in dentistry, family business in marketing, or favourite play in the theatre.' Instead of a theory, he suggests setting tasks arising from 'a model, proof, procedure, test or experiment.' For example, he asks students of psychology to 'select one of the ten personality theories listed in the course outline [and] apply it to your own personality. Evaluate the theory using yourself as the subject. What are its strengths and weaknesses with specific reference to your own personality? What, if any, is the applied value of this specific personality theory?'

Quoted in Hanlon (2002) in *Focus on University Teaching and Learning*, 11:3, the in-house journal for Dalhousie University

When problems produce only one answer, they could be individualised after they have been completed by asking students to compare their solution with one you provide, perhaps explaining which one is more effective. By providing a range of incomplete or erroneous answers, you increase the variation of responses.

Finally, the whole task might be individually negotiated. McDowell and Brown (2001) advocate finding ways so:

> ... students are working towards divergent rather than convergent goals, by use of, for example, individualised negotiated assessments. Where students are meeting tutors over a period of time to discuss evidence of their achievement of required learning outcomes along individual pathways, it is difficult for them to produce anything which is not their own work.

They suggest that learning contracts can be used as a way of asking students to track what they learn and to establish an agreement between tutor and student.

Integrate assessment tasks

Think about:

- if students plagiarised some of the assessment, would that missing learning impact on their ability to do the rest of the course?

- if not, would that matter?

When able students were asked why they did not copy others' essays or download material, some referred to fear of detection. Others were confident they could do a better job than the 'stolen' essay. However, most said they didn't take shortcuts because coursework was necessary to their understanding. They knew they would need to demonstrate this understanding in another context, perhaps an oral presentation or in an exam. So whilst they looked at others' essays and admitted they often reproduced the structure, they wove in their own facts and arguments in order to 'get your head around it'. (Carroll, personal communication, 2001).

When asked why his department had no cases of plagiarism in the past year, a lecturer in a technical subject responded:

'Maybe it's because we know all the students but it's more likely because tasks don't lend themselves to cut-and-paste off the Web and copying is obvious. Students understand that coursework prepares them for exams and in statistics, we individualise work (i.e. same problem, different data).'

When coursework and exams crosscheck and reinforce each other, make this explicit – otherwise only the more strategic and successful students will spot the connection. Linking exams and coursework explicitly also raises the overall status of coursework. Research shows (Bannister and Ashworth 1998, p. 238) that students regard exams as:

> ... powerfully symbolic, with those occurring at the end of a period of study necessarily carrying a sense of dramatic climax. The perceived formality of the examination as an Occasion [sic] lends it gravity, as does its atypical and staged nature.

Assessment is covered in some detail in Chapter 3 because it is fundamental in deterring and dealing with plagiarism.

Build in overt structure to track student progress

Think about:

- how do you feel when a student submits a large piece of work like a thesis or dissertation that you have never seen until that moment?

- what do you currently do to ensure this is the student's own work?

'Richard' told journalists that essay banks are 'like a Napster for essays and coursework ... Usually it's just if someone has forgotten to do the work or has missed a deadline, then they will download and hand it in.'

Grossman (2002)
'All their own work?',
The Independent
15 April 2002, p.11

Structure encourages all students to be as organised and strategic as the good ones. Evans (2000) opines that 'readers tend not to cheat and cheaters tend not to read' so designing in requirements to read and record the reading is likely to help. Designing in staging posts and requiring students to submit work for formative assessment will encourage forward planning. Several studies show that cheating and plagiarism are more common amongst weaker students with poor time-management strategies (Roig and de Tommasco, 1995; Bannister and Ashworth, 1998). Asking in stages to see and initial a plan, a draft and a final product can be helpful because last-minute panic may make plagiarism seem the only solution. (Worried academics, faced with this idea, need to remember that checking that something exists is not the same as assessing it.)

Using assessment to deter plagiarism

3

This chapter considers assessment issues and should be considered in conjunction with the issues raised under course design in Chapter 2. In general, suggestions focus on what you assess and how you manage the assessment process. It also discusses how you might structure tasks to ensure students understand what you want and to lessen opportunities for copying.

Giving students specific instructions

Harris (2001, p. 44) asserts:

> … clarity helps students understand what is expected of them and encourages them to do their own work because they feel more confident about exactly what to do … a major source of poor student papers (not just plagiarising) is the unclear assignment.

If you cannot tell whether your instructions are clear, you could ask a colleague to comment; student feedback can also help when assessing and revising instructions. Even things which you take for granted might confuse students. Being explicit is especially important for some students such as international students who are not always used to decoding implied task instructions. I remember a colleague telling a story about a student in an exam interpreting the instruction to 'discuss' as an invitation to ask their neighbour, 'What do you think?'. The student did so – loudly.

Specific instructions also discourage students from reusing their own previous work (technically known as duplication).

As well as being specific about how students must approach the task, especially where collaborative learning might be involved, you could specify how students should designate shared work as distinct from individual contributions. For example, you might ask them to:

- write a preface describing who did what in a group report;

- cite each other in jointly written work just as they would library sources;

- use a device such as different colours to demarcate individual contributions in a shared artefact such as a poster; or

- conduct their discussions online using a threaded discussion package which dates and times individual contributions.

You could also use the activity on page 19 to ensure they are all thinking about collusion in the same way.

Using a signed statement of originality

In many institutions, students are routinely asked to sign (or better, compose and sign) a statement that asserts that the work is original, the result of individual effort, and written by the signatory. If the piece of work has arisen from collaboration, the contributions of each person could be acknowledged and described in an opening statement.

One example of a disclaimer

Students at Ruskin College in Oxford must submit a form with each piece of written work that includes an individualised statement that this particular work is their own, writing in the name of the paper, what it is for and who they are rather than simply signing a standard form. This is a fairly common requirement. What makes this form special is that it also includes a one-and-one-half page 'tutorial' on correct paraphrasing and use of quotes. The form includes a sample text, an unacceptable rewriting of the original and three different ways in which the original could be used acceptably . The students thus have an opportunity, again and again during their programme, to learn these skills.

A statement might draw attention to specific rules and aspects that the marker views as essential as in this suggested wording (Harris, 2001 p. 60):

> I hereby affirm that (1) the research and writing of this paper are entirely my own; (2) I have not intentionally plagiarised any portion of this paper but have used quotation marks and citations appropriately; and (3) I have not helped any other student inappropriately by lending my notes, papers, disk, files or other materials.

Of course, many students sign such statements without thinking, just as most of us click the box saying we have read the agreements governing transactions before carrying out procedures online. However, asking for a signed statement or a completed checklist of requirements might be one more link in the range of interventions which as a whole, could have an impact.

> **Think about:**
>
> * if you decided to start using a statement, who would need to be involved in the decision?
>
> * how would you inform the students about the purpose of the statements?

Asking for drafts

Academics say they are uneasy when a piece of work, especially one that carries a lot of academic weight like a dissertation or major project, arrives fully formed on their desk. How can they be sure the student him or herself was the author? Some pieces of work are large enough to warrant asking for drafts and if so, this either deters wholesale copying or lessens last-minute panic, a major cause of plagiarism. Soliciting drafts also helps students learn that good writers edit and revise their work using feedback from other students or from teachers. A more minimalist approach is to ask for drafts to be submitted alongside the final piece of work. Their existence is a reassuring sign of student effort.

Drafts for learning and deterrence

A course in geography originally required two essays, one towards the beginning of the course and one near the end. The tutor became increasingly despondent that despite all the time and effort spent marking and writing comments on the first essay, invariably there was little improvement in the second. The course now requires only one [essay]. First, students write a draft by a given date. In a seminar session, they are paired up and give detailed feedback to their partner who then redrafts the essay. When the essay is finally submitted it is accompanied by an account of how the feedback has been used, e.g. 'I've included more sources because the first draft was criticised for using only two. I've kept the introduction the same even though it was criticised as unclear because I don't agree…'.

As a result of this change the tutor has halved his marking load. It is true that only one topic is now assessed rather than two as before but the tutor believes that educationally this is more than compensated for by the following benefits:

* it develops the students' critical faculties;

* significantly better work is produced; and

* it is more like the 'real world' – good writing involves redrafting in the light of criticism.

[and it would deter plagiarism].

Rust (2001), LTSN Generic Centre publication

Asking students to assess each other using the teacher's criteria has many benefits including increasing the number of people keeping an eye out for plagiarism as in the example below:

Peer review to improve learning and spot plagiarism

A computing studies lecturer, faced with classes that doubled and doubled again in size, stopped marking essays himself. Instead, he instructed students to submit their work electronically, removed their names, assigned each student three essays to mark and provided the marking criteria. Students were then marked on the quality of the feedback they provided and how well they used the marking criteria. Several unexpected benefits ensued. The students were pleased their work was 'marked properly'(!), they wrote better essays themselves the next time, and they identified plagiarism in the unnamed scripts. Anonymity was crucial to calling attention to cheating.

Davies (2004)

Assessing the process as well as the final product

Even in a standard task, how the student arrives at an answer might vary even if the final result is largely similar. Sometimes the process is as relevant as the final answer and can, therefore, provide a more individualised artefact for assessment. In group work (which is a valuable learning tool and not one to be abandoned lightly), one way to deter collusion is to use the group activity to provide the learning but not as a sole source of assessment because communal effort can easily be exploited by freeloaders. If you choose to use group projects leading to assessment, think about:

- **requiring an individual record of what the group did**. This could be captured in contemporaneous logs (monitored, dated and initialled to ensure they are not made up the night before submission). Asynchronous online discussions produce a dated record of individual input for later review. Even minutes of group meetings usually show members' contributions.

- **asking for individual retrospective reflections on the group's work**. Log entries of group activity, rather than assessment *per se*, could provide material for individual writing on topics such as each person's contribution to the project (perhaps written under supervision, which allows you to compare answers for consistency and includes examples). Individuals could assert and illustrate their own learning arising from the project or evaluate the group's product (whatever it might be). A retrospective analysis of the problem-solving strategies used by the group (with examples from the group's experience, perhaps drawn from the log) can often cover very similar outcomes to the project itself. You could then allocate marks to reflect the relative importance of any one of these writing tasks for the student's final grade.

Setting criteria for assessment that take collaboration into account

Chapter 4 describes how one lecturer, in an effort to encourage collaboration and discourage collusion, stated clearly what was and was not acceptable. Here, the suggestion is to reward individuality and unique solutions by specifically mentioning them in assessment criteria. It is also helpful to state clearly whether assessment will take into account both the content and the language in which it is expressed. If not, is it acceptable for students to ask others to edit their work for grammar and vocabulary? You will help all students if you spell this out and you will especially address concerns of international students.

Reconsidering essay titles

Essays can be an effective and reliable way of assessing learning outcomes and the ability to write essays is seen as a valuable skill in its own right, particularly in some disciplines. However, because of their ubiquity and their long-standing popularity, academic essays are also more prone to plagiarism than other forms of writing. The essay banks and so-called paper mills described in Chapter 1 contain tens of thousands of possible titles offered for sale or for free. Both wholesale downloading and cut-and-paste plagiarism are possible and according to some, provide a real threat to final awards.

If you use essays, general or standard topics such as an essay on George Eliot, Napoleon or genetically modified food could be individualised (for example, by asking students to compare how an Eliot character and a recent public figure of their choice dealt with a situation). Because essay sites date quickly, asking for a recent event to be considered will greatly lessen cut-and-paste opportunities (for example, discussion of the impact of recent legislation on GM foods). Another way to narrow topics is to ask students to write about what did not happen. McKenzie (1998) suggests:

> …instead of asking why events turned out particular ways in our past … we might ask students to hypothesise why various outcomes did not occur [or] pose questions that have never been answered.

This kind of task will inevitably produce more variety and will probably mean it is easier to spot collusion.

Create engaging assessment tasks

Students are often demotivated by carrying out academic work which seems to be purely routine, such as lab reports which have been done by many students before them, using the same equipment, with identical 'findings'. In this situation they can feel that there is nothing for them to contribute and that they are simply going through the motions … In comparison, students do value and take seriously assessment which appears to have some meaning … for example where they can see that they are developing skills and knowledge which will be relevant outside the university, or where they can express some choice and individuality in their work.

McDowell and Brown (2001, p. 7)

Using defined requirements and narrow task specifications

Furedi (2000) suggests that teachers 'demand that students engage with the literature provided by the course convener' as a way of deterring plagiarism. Harris (2001), in a very comprehensive and useful online paper 'Anti-plagiarism strategies in research papers', suggests being very specific about requirements as in '… the paper must make use of two Internet sources, two printed book sources, two printed journal sources, one personal interview and one personally conducted survey' (p. 4). (Note: this very demanding set could be modified, of course, for lesser pieces of work!) Harris (2001) also mentions instructions such as:

- use one or more sources written within the past year;
- use one or more named books/articles; and
- incorporate the information provided [by the lecturer] such as data or cases.

You might alter the task by asking students to use a mix of primary and secondary sources of information. Boehm (1998) suggests asking students to use interviews, surveys, questionnaires, email correspondence with experts and/or actual experience like attending a workshop as well as the more standard secondary sources when constructing an essay or research paper.

One simple way to check that a student's writing arose from research and reading would be to ask students to submit photocopies of the four or five most useful sources used in creating the report or essay. This is no problem for the student who writes his or her own paper and a headache for those who copied it.

Insist the students engage with the literature

Gregory Hanlon (2002) from the Department of History selects two research articles on a related topic and asks students to encapsulate the authors' arguments, note the means they used for reaching conclusions and explain why he (Hanlon) put them together. He requires students to avoid 'moralising' and to make their case in five pages (c. 2,500 words). Hanlon claims the exercise, 'obliges students to write, rewrite and rewrite' and alerts them to the use of sources in history whilst avoiding 'making moral pronouncements on past societies' rather than being analytical. Critical material in all disciplines makes this assignment adaptable in fields other than History.

One teacher, fed up with students copying from each other in a course teaching computer-assisted design, asked them to also make the object and submit it along with the design. He claimed that in the three years since they made this change, no students had copied because seeing two identical objects was instantly recognisable in ways that two identical designs apparently were not.

Using other methods of recording learning for assessment

Instead of an essay, you might ask for:

- **an annotated list of sources** – the list could be accompanied by comments on, for example, the reliability of the source, how the information was used in the group project, or how it is relevant to the topic;

- **an outline** rather than a finished product or a list of the resources that **would** have been useful (had the document been written) – both can go a long way towards showing understanding and knowledge;

- **skills-based** assignments where students must produce evidence of their competence;

- assignments that revolve around **case studies or scenarios**; Gajadhar (1998) claims these offer fewer opportunities for plagiarism; or

- **reflective journals and critical incident accounts** that record the student's own experience and that can 'be triangulated by [evidence from] a practice tutor or workplace mentor' (McDowell and Brown, 2001 p. 6).

You might also ask students to construct and display posters. This form of assessment encourages students to summarise, structure and select information.

Tracking the programme as a whole will ensure students **do** practise and perfect valued academic writing skills but most students demonstrate many times that they can write essays before graduation. Asking for different kinds of work can significantly lessen the chances of submitted work being bought, faked or copied. More importantly, many of the above assessment methods are linked with deep learning and higher motivation so this is probably a win-win situation where both you and the students benefit.

Use skills-based assessments

A lecturer on a teacher training course attributes the low rates of plagiarism to several things including:

'drumming away at the need to reference. But mostly, it's due to asking students to write most assignments linked to their practice which, because it is often observed by tutors and school mentors, can easily be cross checked.'

Using assessment to verify authenticity

To check that the student's work has actually been done by the student rather than bought, copied, downloaded or recycled, you might organise:

- **a random viva of a percentage of the students.** If students know about this in advance, it might help deter some from attempting plagiarism. Oral exams can quickly identify whether or not students are able to talk about ideas and concepts covered in their work. They can also show that students who may not readily generate quick responses in class can discuss ideas they have had time to think through and organise in written form. However, if a viva suggests that a student might not be as familiar with the work as you would expect – perhaps because he or she is unable to explain technical or unusual words ('Tell me more about what you meant by iterative re-evaluation of the technological input.') – you may be moving from checking learning to checking suspicions of cheating. Comments on page 83 may become important at this point.

- **an open-book test.** Open-book exams will of necessity push students to use knowledge gained through other activities in the course rather than reproduce it from memory or from copying.

- **an in-class or supervised task.** Evans (2000) suggests a meta-essay, written under supervised conditions on an undisclosed topic (for example, *Why I structured the essay in this way, Which sources were particularly useful, How I would do it differently next time, What I learned from writing it*). As well as checking authorship, a meta-essay encourages reflection and analysis. Alternatively, you could organise some of the sessions as supervised work time or observed activity.

Meta-essays

_____

Diane Christian Boehm (1998) in her article, 'About plagiarism, pixels, and platitudes', describes how she asks students to write about their work as well as hand it in. She says, 'This reflection piece has in fact become one of my favourite parts of a writing assignment, for it gives me insights into my students' thinking and, since it is not graded or evaluated, creates a wonderful opportunity for dialogue about their development as writers.'

_____

Informing students

4

Informing students about institutional requirements and academic conventions is a necessary (but not sufficient) step in ensuring they can comply with them. Actively teaching the skills is also usually needed and the next chapter will consider how you might teach students how to comply with copyright, to paraphrase properly, to cite others' ideas, and to abide by institutional requirements. This chapter is about how you might alert them to the need for any of these skills.

Think about:

- where and when do your students currently find out about plagiarism?

- is there any evidence that the current situation is ineffective?

- if there's no evidence on the current system, how might you find out if it's working?

Providing students with information about plagiarism is not easy. The information often has to compete with the mix of trivial and significant information that characterises the start of many programmes, and sometimes it is hard for students to judge which information is important. Students receive literally piles of documents or thousands of pieces of information at the start of a three-year degree programme and somewhat less for many postgraduate courses. One university has to ask the local municipal bin men to remain on standby to clear up discarded documents as students leave Freshers' Fairs and induction events for the Underground station. Students, like most of us, only attend to information when they need to – if then – so much induction is ignored.

Despite the relative ineffectiveness of providing information about plagiarism at induction, when sanctions are applied, many institutions tell students 'It's in the handbook' and report the comment is usually met with protests that the alleged plagiariser didn't understand the rules. It is probable that recent human rights legislation makes this situation contrary to natural justice and fairness, i.e. legally unacceptable. Even if this is not the case, it is no longer tenable under UK Quality Assurance Agency (QAA) codes of practice nor, in England, acceptable to the Office of Independent Adjudicators who receive unresolved student complaints.

Honing induction information

Induction sessions on plagiarism are usually brief – you may have only 15 minutes in a 'talking heads' type day or a portion of the first session in the programme to get the message across. Written information (either paper or Web-based) has the benefit of being accessible at any time but may make it even harder to capture students' attention. Whichever medium is used, you need to ensure the crucial facts are stated. Here are some suggestions:

- Link academic conventions to the values that underpin them. This helps to give students positive statements about what they are expected to do, not just negative ones of what they must not do. You might talk about a shared community of ideas and about respecting others' words and/or work in the same way as one might respect their more tangible possessions. Without understanding the basis for academic conventions, students see them as a form of good manners, like eating with the correct fork, or even as traps designed to catch them out. Although they may never embrace these values (and the studies on student motivation referred to in Chapter 1 show this is often the case), students can at least be introduced to the assumptions that form the basis of academic culture.

- Stress the link between good marks and attributing ideas and referencing before mentioning punishments. In university study, being able to find and use others' ideas to support your own argument is highly valued and students' marks will reflect this in ways that were perhaps less explicit in their previous education. A-level students, for example, are often trained for an exam where the rewards come for remembering and writing down a viewpoint, idea or fact but not necessarily for saying where it came from.

- Define and describe plagiarism and collusion without alluding to possible difficulties with the definition. A definition like:

> submitting someone else's work as your own, for academic credit

may seem self-explanatory but studies show this is not the case.

'While students appear to understand what plagiarism is and believe, in many cases quite strongly, that it is morally wrong, once you probe that understanding there can be confusion about what really constitutes plagiarism and what the university and individual tutors will find acceptable. Only providing information on referencing systems does not tackle this confusion.'

(Freewood, 2001)

- Tell students where they can go for more help and information. This may be the most important message of all. They are unlikely to attend to information about academic conventions until they need to, perhaps when they produce a piece of work. Where can they check assumptions:

    - in the handbook?

    - with a personal tutor?

    - on a Website, either the institution's or a generic site such as the Plagiarism Advisory Service offering (www.jiscpas.ac.uk)

    - in specialised handouts, perhaps from a student services department or the library?

    Ensure you also mention learning support staff, teachers of English for academic purposes, or peer tutoring arrangements with more experienced students if these are provided by your institution.

Use activities to underline your message

I followed up a presentation that was given to 100 first-year students at induction and found that, six months later, they remembered the session for how they felt about hearing the information, but not what was said (Carroll, 2002). This does not mean the presentation was wasted effort – students may need many reminders and all opportunities should be used. However, even a brief exercise that asks them to use the definition would reinforce the message at induction. Here are some ideas for doing this:

1. Present cases like the following and ask which describe plagiarism:

    Case 1 – a student asks a friend to see her essay, notes down the structure and jots down the main idea in most of the paragraphs. She then goes home and writes her own essay based on the lecture notes.

    Case 2 – a student writes an essay full of quotes from other authors with each one credited.

    Case 3 – a student downloads four paragraphs from the Web, writes down the Website after the section and includes the four paragraphs verbatum in a three-page paper. No quote marks.

2. Ask students to do the 'draw the line' exercise below:

Where do you draw the line?

In the examples below, number 1 is plagiarism and number 6 is not. Where do you draw the line?

1. Copying a paragraph verbatim from a source without any acknowledgement.

2. Copying a paragraph and making small changes – e.g. replacing a few verbs, replacing an adjective with a synonym and including the source in the list of references.

3. Cutting and pasting a paragraph by using sentences of the original but omitting one or two and putting one or two in a different order, no quotation marks; in-text acknowledgement e.g. 'Jones, 1999' plus inclusion in the reference list.

4. Composing a paragraph by taking short phrases of 10 to 15 words from a number of sources and putting them together, adding words of our own to make a coherent whole; all sources included in the reference list.

5. Paraphrasing a paragraph with substantial changes in language and organisation; the new version will also have changes in the amount of detail used and the examples cited; in-text acknowledgement e.g. 'Jones, 1999' and inclusion in the reference list.

6. Quoting a paragraph by placing it in block format with the source cited in text and list of references.

Based on an exercise in *Academic Writing for Graduate Students* by John M. Swales and Christine B. Feak, University of Michigan (1994).

3. Ask new students to create scenarios, either in small groups or as a whole to illustrate the definition, based on imagination or instances they have encountered; for example, given the word 'duplication', they might produce: 'Andy wrote a paper for a first-year course that got a good grade and submitted the same paper in year three where it got a C.'

4. Do a brief version of the exercise like that described on page 62 asking students to link words/phrases like incorrect referencing, plagiarising, creating data or colluding to descriptions of students' actions.

5. Ask students to create answers for some FAQs like these:

    - Why can't I use the textbook author's words if they are better than any I could think of?

    - What difference does it make if I just put it in the bibliography?

    - It is my work. I've changed the words in the article to my own. Isn't that enough?

    - There are that many opinions out there that somebody has already thought of whatever I might write. If I say something that is original and somebody else somewhere has already come up with it, will I be done for it?

Think about:

- do you specifically mention collusion with students?

- is there any evidence they find this concept confusing?

- are you clear in your own mind what constitutes collusion?

Defining collusion and informing students

Whereas many staff and students find defining plagiarism difficult (see Chapter 1), almost *everyone* has difficulty identifying where collaboration stops and collusion begins. More often than not, students are given instructions such as, 'Work in a group but each of you must submit your own work.' It is relatively common to see peer instruction valued in class only to have students meet with dire consequences when they use it in assignments. Most find this confusing and need clear guidelines and clear definitions. Comments on collusion throughout this Handbook might help you construct guidelines for your own students or you might build on an example like the one on page 44, created for a masters-level course with a very high percentage of non-native speakers of English, or try the exercise on page 19.

Case study on informing students about collusion

'I always include hands-on stuff on collusion but don't call it that. Usually, I call it "Acceptable English language editing and correction for written assessments". I provide a handout specifying what is acceptable and what is not acceptable (see below). We then examine specific cases and I finish by showing the students how they can cite each other in their work just as they would cite books in the library.'

A UK lecturer on a postgraduate course

Handout:

It is acceptable to:

- ask for help from other students or people outside the course in improving your written English language;

- ask friends or other students for comments on work you do not submit for a mark;

- ask others for feedback in practice writing sessions;

- ask for general comments on your strengths and weaknesses in written English;

- approach the English Language Centre on campus, to use their services, and attend their training; and

- self-assess your own work through looking at that of others.

In this course is not acceptable to:

- ask someone outside the course to read and correct written work you intend to submit as your own, even if the corrections are only confined to the English language components of the work – both content of the work and the way in which you write about the ideas must be your own work; or

- submit work for assessment that is not your own – submitting work that is done jointly by you and by others is collusion.

Continuing to offer information

Information about what constitutes plagiarism and how to conform to good academic practice needs to be offered throughout a student's academic career using course handbooks, dissertation cover sheets, assignment briefing sheets, and user-friendly leaflets. Some postgraduates as well as the more strategic undergraduates find that institutional instructions on referencing and definitions of plagiarism are effective (although students from both these groups have told me they would have welcomed more specific instruction on citing Websites, noting these sites frequently change or die). Where no guidance existed, these students said they reverted to whatever rules applied in their discipline-based journals. They recognised the importance of using correct citations outside the university as there are few spotters of published plagiarism more vigilant than the original author.

Diagnosing the level of student need

Where academic writing skills are particularly important, you may want to invest time and effort at the induction stage into checking students' skills and ensuring they have a realistic sense of their own abilities. An online self-testing or self-teaching package could be useful, either created by the institution or using a generic site such as the Epigeum site http://www.epigeum.co.uk/plagiarism Many higher education institutions provide extensive Web-based programmes on plagiarism, such as the site managed by The University of Leeds www.ldu.leeds.ac.uk/plagiarism.

Many include exercises or quizzes, such as:
http://education.indiana.edu/~frick/plagiarism

or you might put some of the exercises in this Handbook online. A growing number of institutions require students to log on and complete the activities in the first three weeks of their course. Others make it a requirement before students can receive a grade for the first piece of work in the first term.

Another approach is to solicit samples of students' work when they first arrive. Students often complain that they receive no feedback on whether or not their writing is acceptable until they are graded on it. Early practice, perhaps using peer assessment, is often welcome, offering the chance to use assessment criteria, marking each others' efforts or trying out exercises such as the suggestions on checking others' citations (see page 63). Of course, the teacher could see practice work and comment on it rather than asking students to check each others'. This has two disadvantages: less learning for students and more

We had one lecturer in the first year who really spelled out what to do and what not to do about plagiarism in the course handbook. There were rules, examples, even a bad example. I kept that handbook beside me for the next three years when I was writing something. It was crucial.

Final-year student

work for teachers. A middle ground might be to sample the students' efforts and provide general feedback to the group along the lines of 'many of you missed examples of paraphrasing that should have been cited.' A practice exercise might help students see that academic regulations apply to them in their writing, not just to a theoretical situation.

Encouraging fellow academics to become interested in plagiarism

I assume because you are reading this book that you are interested in plagiarism. However, you may need to encourage fellow academics or students to also take an interest in the issues and skills described in this Handbook. Some of the activities described below would work best in a group; all are designed to spark interest or alert others to the need to pay attention to plagiarism:

- **give examples of quotes from students using cheat sites** – many have discussion boards attached that serve as chat rooms or collect quotes from this book;

- **use cartoons** or news clippings – a quick search on Google will produce recent online stories; or

- **organise a virtual tour of paper mills** – this could be unstructured individual exploration or something more organised like a 'treasure hunt' exercise ('find an essay on Emily Bronte as a feminist writer') with prizes for the first to produce a result.

I found that, again and again in disciplinary interviews, accused students acknowledged that their attention has been drawn to University regulations, and to the relevant scholarship. The problem is that when offences are committed, students are not relating regulations to their own behaviour, because they have no dishonest intent. They do not see citation conventions as essential devices ... but as niceties on a par with punctuation.

An experienced academic charged with disciplining students accused of plagiarism

---

Think about:

- if you used any of these suggestions, when might they be appropriate?

- who do you need to approach to discuss induction matters?

- who could work with you on this?

Teaching the skills

5

The previous chapter discussed how a short session on avoiding plagiarism might be handled. Such a session, often offered as a lecture to a large number of listening newcomers, has obvious limits in tackling plagiarism. A short talk may be effective at conveying information, but cannot change attitudes and beliefs or develop skills (Bligh, 1998). Many academics explain the prevalence of misuse of paraphrasing and referencing by claiming that students do not know how to reference. Many have been taught that it is perfectly acceptable to copy and thinly paraphrase work from secondary sources. You will need to get students actively involved and devote time to discussion if you wish to overcome the misconceptions and lack of awareness that most students bring to higher education.

Think about:

- how do your students currently learn about plagiarism?

- which students find this sufficient?

- which students need more help?

Induction or apprenticeship?

One way to cope with students' early confusion might be to apply a period of exemption, allowing first-year students (for example) to learn and practise referencing skills and labelling shortfalls as 'poor academic practice'. Certainly many institutions offer students an informal apprenticeship during which those who plagiarise warrant a comment in feedback ('this should be referenced or it will lose you marks'). Some students may even be offered the opportunity to correct the work and resubmit – this is, in effect, a reward as it offers them an extension. I have heard academics justify this state of affairs as necessary owing to students' weak writing skills, their rudimentary awareness of referencing and inexperience in reading for research purposes. Staff claim that asking too much too soon discourages students and lecturers alike, often stating, 'If we're too strict, everyone will fail.'

Other academics (and some institutions) take the view that using others' ideas as one's own for personal benefit constitutes plagiarism no matter when it happens or who is doing it. A senior manager in one university that operates a 'no grace period' told me that almost all students claim their plagiarism was unintended and resulted from misunderstanding of the rules, with PhD candidates being among the most vociferous in this regard. My own university takes the view that ignoring plagiarism, even for what looks like benevolent reasons, encourages students to put off learning about referencing and paraphrasing. We even worried that some would see losing a few marks as a price worth paying for an easier life in their first year. Delay also reinforces the view that academic rules are more about avoiding punishment or being polite than they are about upholding the values of academic discourse. If universities constitute a community of thinkers who build on and acknowledge each other's ideas and if students are junior members of that community, then letting students 'break the rules' whilst offering guidance for the future is inconsistent with academic values and therefore wrong. Plagiarism avoidance is as important as any other academic skill we wish students to develop.

Delaying action on plagiarism is probably ineffective as well as misleading. Studies show that many students don't collect coursework once they know the mark they have been given and do not read corrections and feedback on their work. Those who do receive feedback seem rarely to adapt their practice to comply with well-meaning advice or to correct previously held incorrect ideas. One study (Fritz et al, 2000) explains the ineffectiveness of this feedback by claiming that the effort and time that went into making the error was more memorable and significant to the student than the subsequent correction. Treating all plagiarism as unacceptable means students use the early years to learn the skills rather than delaying until it 'matters'.

It is important to remember that plagiarism can be identified without implying maximum penalties for offenders. The question 'is it plagiarism?' is separate from the question, 'what happens as a result?' See Chapter 7 for suggestions about determining fair punishments, especially at the start of programmes.

Think about:

- are the skills students need to avoid plagiarism actually taught in your programme?

- if so, where does this happen?

Teaching academic conventions

It can be problematic to find time to teach students how to avoid plagiarism, especially in modularised programmes. Compulsory modules are likely to be 'full' of discipline-specific content, but confining teaching to optional modules would mean students either miss it or encounter it several times. To cope with this difficult problem, many programmes default to implicit strategies, expecting students to pick up the skills as they go along. Happily, the more strategic do so. It may also be that the growing emphasis on explicit learning outcomes and on informing students more clearly about all their responsibilities will help all students teach themselves these skills. However, those who read very little, who come from a background where different writing skills were rewarded (see Chapter) or those whose skills are poorly developed for whatever reason will need practice to master academic writing skills. 'Stressing the dire consequences of failing to observe official guidelines, in the absence of constructive and positive guidance, may have a "crippling" effect on the academic confidence of students' (Bannister and Ashworth, 1998, p. 239).

Below are some alternatives to the trial-and-error approach:

1. **making the skills a compulsory element of the programme** – for example, by devising a compulsory first-year module on academic writing in the students' own discipline area which includes practice in citation and acceptable paraphrasing;

2. **offering a compulsory generic course on study skills**, often broadening the syllabus to include writing for academic purposes, library use etc. – for example, all students in one higher education institution in the Midlands must complete a half-module on study skills in their first year, offered at several different times in both semesters; the course content includes academic writing skills;

3. **incorporating skills into discipline-based teaching** – for example, one very large (c.750) Compulsory Introduction to Business course provides a lecture on academic writing then requires a 1,000 word submission in the first month. All seminar leaders spend a morning together marking the papers, looking specifically for referencing and attribution. Where students' work falls below acceptable standards, they attach detailed instruction sheets for correcting the work and require attendance at an additional tutorial.

4. **providing optional academic support and guidance sessions** – for example, through online resources and handouts covering key skills such as time management and advice on avoiding plagiarism; students are usually told of this resource at induction.

How misunderstanding blocks creativity

There are that many opinions out there that at some stage somebody might have thought of ... I have the feeling that if I said something original [the assessor] will say somebody else has said this before you so why haven't you acknowledged them? ... it's a bit worrying about trying to come up with something original.

A first-year student, quoted by Freewood (2001)

Each approach has difficulties. Numbers 1 and 3 risk triggering arguments about diluting content, about where these skills are best taught, and about who is best able to teach them. Generic 'study skills' courses, whilst often championed in programmes that take students from diverse backgrounds, are often seen by students as a distraction from their primary goal of a discipline-based qualification – those most likely to benefit are also most likely to see such courses as an additional burden. Generic 'study skills' teachers struggle with adapting what they offer to a wide range of disciplines and widely variable requirements depending on the contexts where students will use the skills. On balance, designing in compulsory teaching sessions on academic writing and citation skills where students can apply the skills to discipline-specific content as part of their core assessment tasks is the most likely way to ensure students learn and use academic citation conventions.

Many inexperienced students welcome the idea of attending additional instruction in writing for academic purposes in the form of classes, surgeries or drop-in clinics. Help is especially useful if it does not stigmatise the student and is offered at a range of times, as flexible scheduling reduces the chances of compromising students' other work. It is also helpful if the person offering support is a specialist attuned to the needs of particular groups such as mature students, dyslexic students or international students. Supplemental help will need forceful marketing as the students most in need are also those least adept at seeking it out. Resources allocated to this work should reflect the sensitive and often extended nature of this kind of support, especially for international students.

Activities for teaching academic writing skills

To avoid plagiarism, students need to be able to:

- differentiate what needs attribution from what does not;

- use in-text citation conventions;

- create appropriate reference lists and in some cases, bibliographies;

- attribute direct quotes using an acceptable convention such as quotation marks, indented paragraphs, a different font or italics;

- paraphrase and attribute others' words and ideas; and

- use footnotes.

We used to run workshops for students on writing skills but they didn't come. Now we employ a retired academic for four mornings a week to be in the reception area outside the school office. Most who ask for help are international students but anyone can. In the school, he's known as 'the man who sits' and we think this is a better use of scarce tutoring resources.

A UK undergraduate programme leader

Questions show student confusion

One department collected the most common questions they encounter from students regarding plagiarism. The responses demonstrate how difficult students find it to comply with academic conventions. FAQs included:

- Why can't I use somebody else's words if they are better than any I can think of?

- I put the source in the bibliography. Why put it in the text, too?

- What if I can't remember which book I got it from?

- Why use a 'reference'? I said which person had the idea originally.

- I said it was in *The Times*, 1999. Surely that's enough?

- We were taught at school to copy huge chunks out of books. Why is it wrong?

- Does it really matter if I just forget?

- It is my work because I have changed the words in the article to my own so I don't have to reference, do I?

- How closely does one piece of work have to resemble another to be plagiarism?

- How can I not get caught?

Carroll, personal communication, 2001

Students cannot learn how to do these things by listening to lectures which lay out the rules; they need to practise and receive feedback as to whether or not they did so acceptably. Freewood (2001) notes that students often express confidence in their understanding of plagiarism yet once you probe, there can be confusion. Students she interviewed confirmed the need to talk with an academic in a tutorial-type environment where students can ask questions. She also found evidence of the importance of a good relationship with academic staff in helping students raise concerns about plagiarism. In whatever setting you decide to teach these skills, the following activities could be used.

'I know you should be able to go to your teacher and ask about referencing but I never would. If I was going to ask something it would be some big idea from the lecture, not something like referencing which seems more like I'm wasting his time.'

Third-year student

1. To ensure students know the difference between cheating in general and plagiarism and collusion in particular, you might offer a list of behaviours like the one below, based on research done in 1995 by Franklyn-Stokes and Newstead and updated with reference to the Web. All are cheating but only some are plagiarism.

Differentiating cheating behaviours

Ask students to identify which actions would constitute plagiarism, defined as 'passing off someone else's work as your own' and which are examples of collusion, defined as plagiarism where the work is that of a fellow student.

1. Allowing your own coursework to be copied by another student.

2. Taking unauthorised material into an exam.

3. Fabricating references or a bibliography.

4. Lying about medical/other circumstances to get special consideration.

5. Copying another student's coursework with their knowledge.

6. Buying coursework from an essay bank or a 'ghost writer'.

7. Taking an exam for someone else or vice versa.

8. Illicitly gaining information about the contents of an exam.

9. Inventing data (for example, making up answers to a survey).

10. Not contributing a fair share to group work that is assessed for a group mark.

11. Ensuring the availability of books/journals in the library by deliberately mis-shelving them or cutting out chapters/articles.

12. Paraphrasing material from a source without acknowledging the original author.

13. Copying material for coursework ... without acknowledging the source.

14. Copying from a neighbour during an exam.

15. Altering data (for example, making the results of a survey seem more favourable).

16. Doing another student's coursework for them.

17. Submitting jointly written coursework as if it was an individual piece of work.

The list of behaviours above is based on Franklyn-Stokes, A. and Newstead, S. E. (1995).

Note: You could also use this list to check student understanding of other words such as cheating, collusion, plagiarism, impersonation, duplication, and falsification of data by asking them to match the word to the appropriate behaviour.

2. To teach students when they must use a citation, issue students with an academic essay, either written specially for the exercise or obtained by exchanging essays within the cohort. Ask students singly or in small groups to review the work, checking whether or not the rules listed below have been followed.

Citation rules

The statements in bold are offered as rules students must follow. The questions in italics could be used to guide students in reviewing an academic essay.

These must be marked with a citation:

- **direct quotations**
  – does any of it read like it is someone else's words other than the student writer? Has the author indicated direct quotations correctly by using, for example, indented paragraphs, quotation marks or a change of font?

- **paraphrases and summaries of others' ideas**
  – if the writer could not be expected to have created this idea, is it cited?

- **arguable assertions, i.e. anything controversial or not clearly factual**
  – is anything not cited which a student could imagine themselves disagreeing with or debating?

- **statistics, charts, tables and graphs** from any source, even if the writer created the graph using material from another source.

These do need not to be marked with a citation:

- **common knowledge** – if a wide spectrum of readers are familiar with an idea or its truth is generally accepted, you need not cite it; quotations, paraphrases or summaries attributable to a specific source, however, should still be cited if at all possible – no matter how widely known.
  Is anything cited unnecessarily?

- **facts** available from a wide variety of sources – if a number of textbooks, encyclopaedias or general reference sources include an idea you wish to use in your text, you need not cite it; you can still increase your credibility, however, by citing; most statistics should be cited.
  Are any facts not cited that might usefully be so?

- **your own ideas, discoveries or words** (excluding, of course, words based upon another's words or ideas).

Based on information offered to US students on
http://www.bgsu.edu/offices/acen/writerslab/handouts/plagiarism.htm

3. To teach students how to use correct citation conventions, offer examples of acceptable and unacceptable practice such as the following extract from Ruskin College mentioned in Chapter 4:

Unacceptable practice

The material in italics in the following paragraph has been taken from Eric Taplin, *The Dockers' Union*, Leicester University Press, 1985, pp. 166–7. If students use these ideas without a statement of where they come from, as in the version below, this would be plagiarism.

... James Sexton of the National Union of Dock Labourers was a good example of a trade union leader who became a reformist. His *views were moulded by his industrial experience. He always claimed that he was an agitator and a socialist but he was increasingly at home among the reformist trade union establishment. With the foundation of the Labour Party his allegiance to the more radical ideology of the ILP waned. His socialism was never much more than a search for enlightened reforms to better the conditions and standard of living of working people. Such modest aims put him increasingly at odds with the more radical elements within the Liverpool labour movement.* The same story could be told about many other trade union leaders whose careers started in the late nineteenth or early twentieth centuries.

Examples of the proper use of this material would be:

Acceptable practice

James Sexton, the Liverpool dockers' leader, was an example of a trade union leader for whom, 'socialism was never much more than a search for enlightened reforms to better the condition and standard of living of working people.'[1] As a result, when the Labour Party was formed he drifted away from the ILP and its more radical outlook. The same story could be told about many other trade union leaders whose careers started in the late nineteenth or early twentieth centuries.

[1] Eric Taplin, *The Dockers' Union*, Leicester University Press, 1985, p. 167.

or:

Acceptable practice

As Taplin (1985, pp. 166-7) has pointed out about
James Sexton, the Liverpool dockers' leader's:

> views were moulded by his industrial experience. He
> always claimed that he was an agitator and a
> socialist but he was increasingly at home among the
> reformist trade union establishment. With the
> foundation of the Labour Party his allegiance to the
> more radical ideology of the ILP waned. His socialism
> was never much more than a search for enlightened
> reforms to better the conditions and standard of living
> of working people. Such modest aims put him
> increasingly at odds with the more radical elements
> within the Liverpool labour movement.

The same story could be told about many other trade
union leaders whose careers started in the late
nineteenth or early twentieth centuries.

or:

Acceptable practice

James Sexton, the Liverpool dockers' leader, was an
example of a trade union leader for whom socialism
never amounted to much more than an aspiration to
improve the conditions of life for working people,
through reforms. As a result, when the Labour Party
was formed he drifted away from the ILP and its more
radical outlook (Taplin, 1985, pp. 166-7). The same
story could be told about many other trade union
leaders whose careers started in the late nineteenth or
early twentieth centuries.

Bob Purdie, Examinations Officer, Ruskin College, July 1996 (used
with permission)

4. Once students are alerted to ways to cite others' ideas, check they can paraphrase by offering acceptable and unacceptable versions of the same text as in the example below, taken from a site maintained by the University of Alberta Libraries.

Acceptable and unacceptable paraphrasing

This exercise is designed to teach 'proper paraphrasing' using a text by Thomas Flanagan entitled *Riel and the Rebellion: 1885 Reconsidered* and using a convention which numbers citations and lists them at the end of the work. The verbatim text reads:

> *However, the true importance of the Rebellion in our history is more symbolic than military. It will always be remembered because it expressed several of the fundamental tensions of Canada: the aspirations of western settlers to run their own affairs versus the desire of Ottawa to control the public domain according to its own conceptions of the national interest; the conviction of natives, both Indians and Metis, that this was 'their land' versus the belief of Canadians in British sovereignty; the conflicting sympathies of English and French Canadians towards the French-speaking, Catholic Metis; the desire of some in the west for union with the United States; and the quite realistic fear among Canadian statesmen that American annexation would follow if Canada did not have a strong presence on the prairies.*

Two rewrites are offered:

(i)   The importance of the Red River Rebellion is not due to its military aspect but the symbolic one. The rebellion will be remembered because it revealed several things about Canada. First, the rebellion revealed the tension between the need for Ottawa to control the west and the western settlers' need to control themselves, or join the United States. Second, the conflict showed the division between the Natives and the other Canadians who believed in British sovereignty, and the division between the English and French Canadians towards the French-speaking, Catholic Metis. Third, the rebellion revealed the fear of some politicians that the Americans would take over the west if Canada did not settle the prairies.

(ii) The Red River Rebellion will be remembered by what it revealed about the insecurities of a fledgling nation and the conflicts among her people. In the west, the settlers aspired to independence from a domineering government in Ottawa while some of the more radical settlers wished to join the United States. Further conflict existed between the Natives, who viewed the land as theirs, and the Canadians who perceived the land as an extension of British ownership and governance. Other sources of tension were found between the differing English and French perceptions of the plight of the French-speaking, Catholic Metis. Omnipresent during these conflicts was the fear that the United States could readily subsume the Prairies (Flanagan 4).

The student is then asked which is not plagiarism because:

1. proper acknowledgement for the ideas presented in the passage is given; and

2. the writer uses his or her own words.

And which is considered plagiarised because:

1. only the wording of a few phrases was changed and the sentences were only rearranged; and

2. the writer does not acknowledge the source of the information and ideas.

http://www.library.ualberta.ca/guides/plagiarism/

Once students can differentiate between acceptable and unacceptable paraphrasing, ask them to paraphrase brief extracts themselves then check their efforts using peer review. You might suggest non-native speakers of English build in an intermediate step: explaining the text to a friend who writes it down. Moving from written text to speech often removes the strong pull towards using the original authors' phrases and words.

A cursory Google search of plagiarism sites will offer similar activities and guidance.

Helping students understand how academics assess their work

Students who have used and discussed marking criteria are far more likely to use them to guide and shape their own submissions. Price et al (2000) demonstrate that getting students to use criteria themselves rather than just reading them in a course handbook is a key element in ensuring students understand what is valuable in their work. One way to encourage this is to use essay banks and 'cheat' sites to generate essays as these often have very few references. This suggestion is viewed by some academics as provocative, possibly helping students cheat. Others regard it as naïve to believe students are unaware of such 'services', drawing an analogy with arguments against sex education. As well as helping students understand 'the academic game', asking them to mark essays available for sale will demonstrate their generally low quality and high cost (Olsen, 1998). I have looked in some detail at a large number of such sites and find the quality generally very poor indeed. (See also page 44 for peer review exercises.)

Think about:

- how important do you consider spending time on academic writing and avoiding plagiarism compared to all the other things students must master?

- which of your students will need more help than you can offer?

- how can you encourage them to get the help they need?

Reinforcing understanding for particular groups

Some students need to set aside skills and assumptions that served them well in previous educational settings and learn complex new ones. For example, students might have been rewarded for reproducing large chunks of others' texts as a way of signalling they know of the existence of this information (Ryan, 2000). This is especially common in some A-level syllabuses and in international students' previous education. Angelil-Carter (2000, p. 165), discussing the needs of South African students, reminds her fellow academics that these students often:

> … are immersed in highly religious cultures … oral history and [a] literature tradition that requires and values accuracy of memorisation. The student who is plagiarising may simply be making use of the modes of textual construction that he or she knew at school.

Training students to operate as researchers

Teachers hope that training students in research methods will benefit the students themselves. The skills of inferring, deducting, deriving meaning from context, and forming hypotheses have value far beyond their application to scholarly research. If these skills are neglected, de-emphasised or misunderstood, something significant in the educational process will be lost. Technology [can be] misused to create shoddy imitations of responsible scholarship [rather than] a nuanced and judicious selection of sources to produce a coherent and persuasive whole … Instructors can model the process through lectures and guided discussions and can illustrate the difference between the critical use of sources and the arbitrary recitation of random references from a database … When the instructor promotes a climate of authentic ownership of texts and ideas, it will be easier to discuss the differences between genuine scholarship and the mere assemblage of cannibalised references that create the illusion of thoughtful research.

Mirow and Shore (1997, p. 43)

Many international students 'borrow' the words of native authors through lack of confidence in their own abilities to write correct, clear English. Watkins and Biggs (1996, p. 279), commenting on Chinese students, note:

> Students who want to make a point particularly clearly see paraphrasing the source as a strange thing to do when the source itself makes the point better than they ever could reword it in an imperfectly mastered language.

Gathering ideas and quotes from a wide range of sources to construct an argument or evaluate the reliability of the information is valued in the UK but some international students find it both strange and disrespectful, especially if they come from academic cultures where offering personal and possibly critical views is not acceptable.

Setting aside previously successful strategies and learning new ones can take considerable time and effort but where task requirements are made very explicit, many students adapt quickly (Volet and Kee, 1993). Where requirements remain implicit and no help is provided, some struggle for years. Even with explicit information, many need specialist help (Fox, 1994). Many authors of books on teaching in HE address the teaching of international students explicitly, including reference to plagiarism (see, for example, Carroll and Ryan, 2005).

Stages students use to develop their writing skills

Wilson describes four stages of writing that non-English speakers adopt:

- **Repetition**: simple copying from an unacknowledged source. [This happens when the student is] not confident of the content area. **Unacceptable.**

- **Patching**: copying, with joining phrases, from several sources. [This happens when a student offers] some general, non-specific acknowledgement. Still **unacceptable** but harder to spot.

- **Plagiphrasing**: paraphrasing several sources, and joining them; all sources are in the reference list, but pages unspecified. **Unacceptable.**

- **Conventional academic writing**: ideas taken from multiple sources and repackaged to make a more or less original and relational synthesis. Quotes properly referenced, general sources acknowledged. [This happens when the student is] quite confident of what is being said and able to create a new 'package' even if none of the ideas are new.

Biggs, J. (1999), *Teaching for Quality Learning in Higher Education,* p. 129 (OUP) quoting Wilson (1997)

Making the time

Sometimes, it is hard to remember how confusing, challenging and alarming students find these matters, especially if you have been using academic conventions and assumptions successfully for years. You need to plan in time for discussion, practice and feedback as well as for information giving. Active learning methods add to students' knowledge and allow you to identify their misconceptions. However, remember that whatever time you give to this teaching, students will appreciate written guidance and clear regulations for use later. They may also appreciate signposting to sites where such guidance is offered. Your own university may have such a site or you could locate useful ones via a generic site such as that managed by The Plagiarism Advisory Service http://www.jiscpas.ac.uk.

Detecting and confirming a case

6

Detecting and dealing with plagiarism will always be a less attractive option than designing out opportunities and teaching students the skills they need to comply with academic conventions. However, it is likely that, intentionally or unintentionally, students will plagiarise. When that happens, individuals need to act to ensure the integrity of their own institutions' awards and of higher education in general. A holistic approach relies on detection as part of the overall package – ignore it and the rest is less effective.

Detection is actually a process rather than a one-off discovery. Reactive detection begins when a marker wonders, 'Is this the student's own work?' – usually because something in the work arouses suspicion. The reactive detection process, if it continues, moves to further investigation and, eventually, to a decision to continue the case under a disciplinary process or to the decision that no academic misconduct has occurred. This reactive and investigative process is reasonably familiar: academics have followed it with greater or lesser enthusiasm for years. Proactive detection, on the other hand, is a relatively recent phenomenon, offering the possibility of screening students' work rather than waiting for an individual case to crop up. This chapter looks at all of these aspects – suspicion, confirmation and screening – and suggests how you might improve your ability to spot and confirm plagiarism. Subsequent chapters deal with taking action and suggest ways for deciding which actions or penalties are appropriate.

Think about:

- what currently alerts you to possible plagiarism?

- what do you currently ignore (in student work) even though it might be plagiarism and if you do, why?

- what would you never ignore and why?

A threat from over-reliance on detection?

University managers and many busy academics from 2002 onwards watched the rise in the number and capability of bespoke software programs to identify copying and hoped that would be 'the answer'. It was commonplace to see such tools referred to as 'plagiarism detectors', overlooking the less palatable truth that only academics themselves can make such a judgement. Relying on electronic detection also ignored the need for using a wide range of strategies to ensure no one group of students was unfairly targeted or that different kinds of copying or fraudulently generating coursework were not overlooked.

Even if text-matching was 'the answer', it would not make the issue of plagiarism disappear. On the contrary, relying on detection alone could threaten the experience of both staff and students. This is certainly the view of some observers, referring to people who appear interested in catching students as 'the plagiarism police' (Levin, 2006) and even characterising such activity as 'a witch hunt…that amounts to saying "We regard you as potentially dishonest, a cheat and a thief, and we are watching you"'. (Levin, 2004, p. 8).

A search for technological solutions to the worries about student plagiarism is understandable. It is tempting (and apparently fitting) to believe that a problem greatly aided by the development of technology can best be dealt with by similar means. However, there is clear evidence that such an approach is ultimately self-defeating. Cole and Kiss (2000) describe the use of surveillance cameras, silent pagers and tiny video cameras by cheaters in American universities, which in turn leads to lecturers using forensic linguistics to catch them. They call this behaviour a 'dispiriting arms race…reminiscent of James Bond' (p. 6). In fact, like any purely 'catch-and-punish' approach (only more so), it will simply lead to a never-ending 'arms race' between the students and the university.

Under-detection of plagiarism

A student apparently changed every seventh word in a copied document and ran it through the text matching software which did not register it as copied. He then said, 'It was 2500 words long. Took ages! I'll never do that again.' When his story appeared on a mailbase discussion list, it triggered a lively discussion on other ways to bypass software capabilities.

A UK Lecturer

> **Think about:**
>
> * whose job do you believe detection to be?
>
> * what might be the long-term consequences of significant underdetection for the course? For your students? For you?

Evidence suggests that some or possibly even many markers overlook suspicious signs in their students' work, even if they are aware of their possible significance for plagiarism. Many studies (Barrett, 2005; Simon et al, 2003; Lambert et al, 2006) say most markers choose not to 'spot' plagiarism, opting instead for allocating low marks and/or offering feedback on referencing rather than labelling the students' submissions as plagiarised. Markers who do label the work as plagiarism are more likely to use informal approaches (or 'rough justice' as one I spoke to called it) rather than using official channels. Lambert et al (2006) attribute markers' reluctance to 'fear that the allegation could not be substantiated' (p. 496). My own investigations (Macdonald and Carroll, 2006) found that the most common reason for academics not using procedures was concern about the amount of time that would be required, though I regularly hear other explanations too.

Some staff cite an absence of clear teaching on how to avoid plagiarism and see detection as unfair on students generally and as potentially discriminatory against international students. For others, pointing the finger of blame at some students is viewed as unfair if other students, taught by different staff, are not equally at risk. Some staff, having discovered extensive plagiarism, believe they will be seen as failed teachers compared with those who have not made such a discovery (even if lack of detection in the latter case arises from a failure to look). Finally, I have heard many staff complain bitterly that their management does not back their wish to pursue a case against a student for plagiarism. These academics claim that instead of offering support, their managers are more worried about the school or university appearing on the front page of the *THES* in a less than flattering light or losing the revenue of a student facing dismissal. Comments in Chapter 8 on institutional policies and culture may go some way towards addressing these worries, as do the sections on establishing a case later in this chapter.

This chapter takes the view that all plagiarism should be dealt with and that individual academics need the skills, time and support to do this job well. A lecturer who identifies plagiarism and does not take action might be contributing to the alleged diminution of academic values that often features in the national press.

Clarke and Lancaster (2006) describe tracking the use of RentaCoder, a site designed to help businesses find computer programmers for small projects. 12% of postings came from students. Half of the student users were described as 'habitual', asking for between four and seven pieces of work. The authors make a case for more automated detection for source code and for redesigning assessments to make 'contract cheating' more difficult.

> **Think about:**
>
> - does your willingness to take action or ignore plagiarism have an impact on your students' motivation to learn?
>
> - if you currently take a relatively relaxed approach to plagiarism, what might influence you to adopt a different approach?

Proactive detection before marking

Proactive detection need not depend on electronic submission or, sometimes, on extra effort. For example, one marker of 30 or 40 papers can usually remember what previous students 'in the pile' have written and link similar ones. Markers often mention the tendency for students who have copied each other's work to hand in papers together, so maintaining the order of submission may also help. However, if you ask yourself the question, 'Should I be looking at any of these papers especially carefully to be sure that the work submitted is that of the student?' then you will probably have to take some deliberate action to find the answer. Some proactive detection strategies have already been described as part of designing courses that deter plagiarism (Chapter 2). Now, in this chapter, their purpose can also be expanded to spotting work that might need authentication as the student's own.

To check if any student's submission warrants more checking, you might set a short test, organise a brief viva, compare students' coursework and examination grades, or require a piece of observed writing. Supervised writing may be especially useful in a large cohort where you are unfamiliar with an individual student's abilities. Even a short task lasting 10 minutes on an unannounced topic ('Briefly describe which sources you found most reliable in writing your essay and why they were so useful', 'Summarise the main argument') allows you to compare the student's two efforts. Depending on the brief you give, the student's efforts might also serve as a kind of 'viva' for understanding.

If you try too hard, all you catch is the clumsy ones and the students will spend more time outwitting you than learning.

A UK lecturer

When people are offered the 'writing about writing' idea in a workshop, they quickly say that differences can be explained – students have less time, are under pressure, and cannot use the capacities of word processing. However, academics who have tried it report they have encountered students who could not explain how they used documents only available in a very obscure place or who could not outline the main legal ruling underpinning their argument. In some cases, the factors mentioned could not explain the gap between the English language skills displayed in the two examples. None of these discrepancies 'prove' the coursework was not the student's work, but they do suggest further investigation. They could also form part of the evidence for a case, should one emerge.

Electronic screening of students' work

> **Think about:**
>
> - if you were to start using electronic detection, what would be the first step?
>
> - who might be interested in working with you on this initiative?

If students submit their work electronically, it opens the door to Web-based screening. It also offers benefits beyond screening, especially if it is done via a university's central computing facility in that it creates a timed and dated record, can be more flexible and accessible for students, smoothes the administrative burdens, and protects assessors from viruses which commonly infect students' discs and CDs. As an aside, electronic submission need not preclude hard copy, since many markers prefer the traditional format.

In the UK, the most widely-used and most positively-evaluated tool for comparing student work with the texts available on the Web is offered via the Plagiarism Advisory Service (www.jiscpas.ac.uk) and goes under the trade name of Turnitin. This text-matching software was developed by a US company in the 1990s and is now used by universities around the world, including a growing number in the UK. In mid-2006, the Plagiarism Advisory Service claimed that over 200 further and higher education providers subscribed to the service.

Turnitin works by creating a template of the student's work and searching for similar text in three databases. It 'looks'

- on the accessible and archived Web

- in a bespoke database created over many years, comprising textbooks, copyright material, subscription journals, academics' own work, etc. (at the time of writing, the database claims to hold over 4 billion items with more being added at an accelerating rate)

- in a database containing all previously submitted work (in 2006, this apparently held close to 50 million items).

Something must be happening at the sharp end. How else can we explain the gap between the number of cases we have (just over 100), the number of students we have (more than 30,000) and the statistics you read all the time about how many students are busy plagiarising? At least if we start doing something, it should be easy to track our effectiveness by checking the records on cases.

A manager in one UK university

To use Turnitin, you need a licence, an electronic version of the student's work, and a few IT skills. Either you or your students must upload the work to the service and within a short time, you or your students (depending on how you set up the program) receive a similarity report. In many institutions, tens of thousands of papers are managed in this way with student uploading presenting little difficulty ('The students just did it. No problem.') although where submission is not built into administrative systems and requires chasing to complete the task, this becomes less straightforward. One academic who attempted to introduce students to uploading noted that 'the hassle factor has been substantial'.

Once submitted, a Turnitin report is generated within minutes (except at times of very high volume such as the end of semesters). A list of the students appears with each individual colour-coded to reflect the degree of overlap between the text submitted and that found on the databases. Where more than 75% of the student's work matches, the student's report icon is coloured red; 50% similarity is denoted by a yellow icon; and a 25% match shows up as a green icon. By clicking on

I teach computing and it's a piece of cake for my students to find a program or commission one, so we now book a lab on hand-in day, ask them to load their work, then make a stated change in their program. Those who wrote it can; those who didn't struggle, and the struggle is pretty obvious. We're not sure but we have done this for two years and the number of strugglers is way down.

A UK academic

Tutors sanguine about the capacity of Turnitin

'… [C]areful management of the submission process was required to ensure both an electronic and a paper copy. This made students aware not only of the sophistication of the detection process, but also of [its] limitations. …[T]he service can stall when it reaches embedded spreadsheets and graphics and only allows a student to submit one file per assignment. Students who lacked sophisticated document production skills often produced a paper assignment from more than one electronic document and…were advised just to submit their largest file. Even those students who presented one document found on occasion that the Turnitin UK engine had successfully processed only a subset of their work. Conscientious students worried about these limitations as they were told and we stressed the importance of electronic submission. At least one student removed offending plagiarized material from his electronic submission [believing] we could not compare paper with electronic versions with a staff/student ratio of 1/25. Until enhancements are made to the service to include digital watermarks…and electronic-only submission with industrial-strength secure printing, then we advise caution.'

Martin and Stubbs (2005)
http://www.ltu.mmu.ac.uk/ltia/issue10/martin.shtml
(September 2006)

an individual student's report, you see a list of the places where similar material was found and you can also ask for a side-by-side layout which compares the two texts (i.e. the student's and the similar source). A marker then needs to inspect the report(s) to check whether the similarity is from unauthorised borrowing or is properly cited. As before, academic judgement is still required to decide if the student has used others' work in an unacceptable way.

Advocates for Turnitin say that it is fast, useful and authoritative. As more and more students and institutions submit work, Turnitin has the potential of providing a national resource. Reviewing each report takes very little time – I often hear people say it takes under a minute in straightforward cases and rarely more than four or five in potentially problematic ones. Of course, in a large class, this adds up and a few cases may take longer.

There are also detractors who resist the seeming inexorable rise of the use of Turnitin (although some of their early objections have now been addressed by developments in Turnitin's capability). Objections include the time required to verify reports, and since most students do not plagiarise, the fact that time spent looking offers no benefit. They note that Turnitin cannot cope with many kinds of copying, since not all texts are included in the databases, hence a 'clean' report does not mean absence of plagiarism. Turnitin can do little about the problems of ghost writing and using translation programs (i.e. where the student finds a text in one language and runs it through a translator). Asserting a causal connection is problematic but the rise in the use of Turnitin closely matches the rise in the number of so-called 'ghost writing sites', along with discussions in the media about their impact. Certainly, the creators of such sites boast that their products 'cannot be detected'. Finally, there is concern about Turnitin becoming a monopoly with one tool so dominant that others are not given due attention or encouragement. Detractors are already unhappy with the costs involved and assert this can only worsen as the market becomes more dominated by a single tool.

There are many other tools for matching text available, and some published assessment of their utility and reliability. This is an area that changes very rapidly and a publication such as this Handbook will date quickly. If you are starting out on a search of text-matching tools and wish to extend the search beyond the ubiquitous Turnitin, your best bet is probably to find the latest additions using one of the meta-search engines, and then to access a specialist discussion group such as that managed by the Plagiarism Advisory Service (www.jiscpas.ac.uk) to ask for others' experience. There is a small but growing literature on how these tools are used, which would also be a useful place to look.

A learning technologist introduced Turnitin in one UK university:

...academics need to register, then we magically appear. It's at this face-to-face meeting that we can start to discuss the alternatives and encourage them to think about the balance between using the software and better information for students. We'll help with the creation of online tutorials for students... This approach is a little time-intensive and people slip through the net, but it does allow us to develop networks and disseminate good practice. We can fill in the gaps once local champions are in place. ...it is useful to see how people use it. For instance, staff wishing to use it for publications, and students as more of a formative learning tool.

The use of Turnitin.com

Under the headline 'The use of Turnitin.com to combat plagiarism is raising passions on Canada's campuses':

'[A student] refused to use Turnitin partly because it reverses the onus of innocent until proven guilty. He also objected to how his work was being used. "I'm indirectly helping a private company make a profit off my paper."

[An educational technologist] says services like Turnitin create an antagonistic atmosphere and do nothing to solve the underlying problem…"I think the assumption tends to be, if we've got software to do this, that's better," but it's far more complicated than that. Some Internet sites, for example, offer "translation" engines that will alter plagiarized texts slightly so that they're less likely to be caught by plagiarism detectors.

The real solution is to educate students properly. "We need to take students in hand and work with them to figure out how to document correctly. I think that real plagiarists are fairly rare and probably there's nothing we can do to stop them. They'll cheat no matter what."'

University Affairs Magazine, April 2004

Turnitin as a teaching tool

Some teachers offer students a chance to submit their draft work to Turnitin and encourage them to use the report as formative feedback. Others ask students to submit their final version, then review the report and include it in their submission of the work itself. This kind of approach can provoke controversy. Some see it as 'teaching them to cheat' or 'teaching them to just make the colour go away'. Advocates argue it provides students with clear evidence of what they must attend to in order to comply with regulations, as well as measuring how well they have cited others' work.

On balance, most users say Turnitin is a useful addition to their repertoire of detection strategies. For more information, see www.jiscpas.ac.uk and follow the links for 'detection'.

Alternative ways to screen for collusion

Electronic submission may be the only way to screen for copying between students in very large classes or when relying on multiple markers. Turnitin will do this as will another tool, CopyCatch Gold, which is designed by a forensic linguist and focuses on the language students use. To use CopyCatch, you load all the students' texts, set a percentage of similarity (usually more than 60% overlap, though you can set a higher threshold) and run the program. In minutes, CopyCatch compares every document with every other document and identifies pairs that exceed your stated threshold. You then inspect the nature of the overlap and judge whether it breaches academic regulations. Because CopyCatch encodes the data, does not compile students' work from previous checks, and remains within the licence-holder's control, it avoids some of the concerns voiced about other tools where the converse is true.

On the down side, CopyCatch is less able to compare texts with outside sources such as the Web or print-based databases (though at the time of writing, this capability was being developed). Licensing is available for individuals, departments and full institutions
(see http://www.copycatchgold.com).

A survey on student's views on using Turnitin

*Green et al (2005) surveyed students' views on using Turnitin before the text-matching tool was introduced.

- **228 respondents anticipated benefits:**
  Avoiding unintentional plagiarism (46%)
  Helping them learn (29%)
  Deterring intentional plagiarism (15%)
  Catching cheats (7%)

- **284 replies mentioned concerns:**
  Being accused of plagiarism that was unintentional (39%)
  Turnitin as a company and its reliability (22%)
  Having text retained in a database (19%)
  'Feeling offended' (6%)
  Increasing students' anxiety level (6%)

The authors singled out Law students' answers as they 'disagreed more strongly about the university using the software' and were 'far more expressive in the written comments…and moral indignation ('This is the greatest threat to student liberty in my time at university, no matter how you try to sugar coat it.')

Students from non-English speaking backgrounds were significantly more positive about introducing Turnitin and felt they would benefit more than other students.

I found it [Turnitin] extremely useful because the first draft was c. 40% others' words. All but five were able to reduce their reliance on others' words and/or ensure acceptable paraphrasing. This time, of the five who failed, only one was due to plagiarism – much fewer than last year.
Both students and tutors found the tool useful so we are making it compulsory next year. Yes, I would continue to use it with students. It had a definite impact on the incidences of plagiarism.

An English as a Foreign Language teacher

Reactive detection: spotting the signs of plagiarism

> **Think about:**
>
> - which groups of students are more likely to be identified under your current detection practices? Which are more likely to be overlooked?
>
> - the percentage of international students penalised as a percentage in the cohort as a whole. Does the former exceed the latter? What might explain this over-representation?

Many academics express confidence in their own ability to detect plagiarism (though less so when it comes to bespoke essay services). The most common strategy they use is looking out for changes in a student's writing style. In a survey of 321 academics, 67% of those surveyed said that terminology and sentence structure were significant, with 72% citing changes within the text as indicative. 63% were suspicious if the writing deviated from the student's expected level and 66% said they looked for 'a feeling of familiarity with the text' (Bull and Collins et al, 2001).

Compiling lists of signs that might arouse suspicion was an early source of advice about plagiarism detection. This reliance on a marker's 'eagle eyes' remains the most common tool despite other recent developments in electronic alternatives. Hinchcliffe (1998) suggests some clues are obvious, not to say blatant, such as:

- URLs left at the top of students' pages;

- strange changes in font and/or layout;

- American spelling (in a non-American student) either throughout a document or in scattered sections;

- bibliographies that only cite material not available locally;

- bibliographic references that are all more than three years before submission, especially in a paper on a topical issue;

- bibliographies that do not reflect the content of the coursework;

- introductions and conclusions written in grammatically incorrect English and not addressing the body of the paper, which is written in flawless, complex English; and

- unusual or highly specific professional jargon in a student starting out in the discipline.

Can you spot eight clues that this is not the student's own work?

This exercise appeared in the *Times Higher Education Supplement* on 28 May 2004 p. 4 and is quoted with permission. The task? '…spot eight clues in this essay and win a bottle of champagne.' The winner found 7. Can you do better? The answers appear at the end of this chapter.

Are GM crops safe?

By A Corner-Cutter

There has been a lot of discussion in the media recently about GM crops and whether they are safe. In my essay I'm going to say that it is wise at the moment not to go ahead with these crops, but it may be ok in the future. However, it is important to distinguish between unwanted environmental changes attributable to a transgene and those caused by other aspects of a dynamic agro-environment (Furlong and Gallen, 2004).

A number of well-documented cases show the dangers of GM. In 2000, a GM corn meant for consumption by animals cross-pollinated with corn destined for Taco Bell taco shells. Despite a rapid recall of the tainted corn products, at least 44 people claimed to have gotten ill after the Starlink contaminated corn, suffering from rashes, diarrhea, vomiting, itching and life-threatening anaphylactic shock.

Some people raise issues of 'naturalness' as a way of expressing worry about what GM means for our relationship with the natural world. They may admit that we already live with considerable human intervention in the environment, but see GM as a 'step too far'. For others it may be the presence of animal genes or of even any gene that could not have reached its destination through 'conventional' breeding techniques (1).

Further concerns are raised about the possibility of genes escaping from modified crops into other plants and PTO maybe making 'superweeds' (see, for example, Hughes and Bryant, 2002). Are we likely to be faced by a future in which previously weak

Politicians have started listening to all these worries but have not decided what is best yet.

Less blatant examples in written work should also make the reader uneasy. For example, coursework that:

- addresses the topic only obliquely or addresses only a small aspect of it;

- is out of character for this particular student, especially if it significantly exceeds the usual level of performance or language;

- closely resembles work submitted by other students.

Further suggestions of what to watch for

Harris (2001) suggests clues such as those cited above and adds suggestions about looking for:

- mixed bibliographies where two or more citation systems are used;

- 'lack of citations or quotations' in a long piece of prose; and

- 'signs of datedness' such as using statistics from a fixed and far off time frame or references to past events as if they were current – for example, an essay that purports to be contemporary might include a phrase about '…the way that photographers pursue the Princess of Wales'.

How to carry out a Google advanced search

Choose a phrase of up to 10 words that strikes you as unlikely to have been written by the student. On the Google homepage, click on the hyperlink to the right of the search box that opens the advanced search facility. Put in exactly the phrase you have identified. (It must include the same spacing, spelling and capitalisation.) If that phrase does derive from a Web page, the resulting list of URLs usually has the likely source in the first few items. Locating the phrase on the site is easiest via the 'cache' button under the site listing; the phrase appears in (highlighted) yellow and can be spotted with a quick scroll of the site.

Plagiarism in computing source code

Culwin et al (2001) reviewed a range of products designed to detect plagiarism in source code, that is, in the code that underpins computer programs (see http://www.jiscpas.ac.uk/images/bin/southbank.pdf). The authors conclude that commercially available packages are effective in detecting plagiarism but are not widely used. A survey conducted at the same time as the product review pointed to much higher levels of plagiarism than are currently being dealt with officially, leading to the authors concluding that many more computing departments could usefully screen students' work using tools such as JPlag and MOSS (an acronym for Measure of Software Similarity). They also note that some departments have developed their own in-house detection tools. At the time of writing (five years later), I regularly hear the same points made by computing colleagues.

Confirming a case

Culwin and Lancaster (2001) describe the detection process as moving from suspicion through investigation to confirming (or, in their words, verifying) the way in which the work is most likely to have been produced. Once the case is confirmed, action can then be taken, as detailed in Chapters 7 and 8.

One way to investigate a possible case is to focus on the student's learning. You (or the person responsible for investigating) might invite the student to a viva where questions are asked about the content. ('You used factor analysis in generating the statistics. Can you talk me through how that works?', 'Briefly outline your case against using NATO troops in Bosnia. Why is that central to your argument?', 'You wrote code to do X. What would you need to do to modify it to do Y?')

An alternative tack is to explore how the text was generated without the student being present. Strategies for doing so include:

- **doing several advanced Google searches** for bits of text that read as if they are written by a skilled and experienced writer in the discipline rather than an HE/FE student;

- **asking the student to email an electronic version** of a word-processed document within a short period of time. If the student is unable to do so, this becomes an additional factor to consider when building a case and could guide you in taking the next steps.

If an electronic version is forthcoming, you might check the formatting – is anything still in html? In a Word document you might look at the 'Properties' function (located in the 'File' menu) to see when the document was created and note the total edit time for the piece of work. A 'clean' properties report might prompt further requests (see below). Finally, you could submit the document to a bespoke service such as Turnitin for a report of similarity.

- **asking to see drafts or copies of significant research cited** in the text (although you may only draw conclusions about absence of either drafts or photocopied articles if you have told students in advance that they must be kept). Where they have been told they must keep drafts and research evidence, inability to show them can be one element in confirming a case.

83

If you call the student in for a discussion, you might:

- **ask how he or she located sources** ('You have used statistics from the Turkish State Library. How did you access them?');

- **ask the student to write about how they did the work**, allowing you to have a sample of the student's writing (albeit one generated under conditions different from that of coursework).

Alternatively, you could ask the library which databases students are using and seek their help in checking for similar text.

Keeping the student informed

Think about:

- what does your institution stipulate you must do when interviewing a student?

- what actions would be sensible prior to asking a student to attend an interview?

Whilst investigations may be done without being explicit about the purpose, it is almost always better to inform the student. Before you speak to a student, you need to be clear what the purpose of the discussion might be. If the case has already been verified (i.e. there is a case to answer) and the interview has the primary purpose of investigating further, you could start by providing the student with a copy of the academic regulations relevant to plagiarism, reading the section or sections aloud and asking if the student has any comment. When a student is interviewed in my institution, where plagiarism is dealt with by an experienced and senior person who holds a position entitled 'Academic Conduct Officer', the student is already aware that a case has been alleged and that the interview is designed to explore the issues and to consider and possibly impose penalties. It nevertheless starts as an investigation (see page 117 for more on this system).

Your institution may already have guidance on who may be considered an appropriate companion or supporter for a student in such an interview, and certainly advice should be sought if a student seeks legal representation at this stage. There are a growing number of institutions reporting that students insist on bringing a solicitor. Anecdotal reports of solicitors' adversarial and aggressive manner are growing. Academics describe demands for proof and threats of dire consequences where allegations are not upheld, leaving them (the academics) feeling intimidated and worried. As investigative interviews usually precede disciplinary cases, and serve to gather evidence in preparing a case rather than pursuing a disciplinary action as described in Chapter 8, legal representation is definitely inappropriate at this stage. In many institutions, regulations state that legal representation is excluded at all stages of the process as these involve legitimate academic judgements. (There is more on matters of academic judgement in the sections below.)

In general, investigative interviews last about 40 to 60 minutes and will require careful notes recording what was discussed and the outcomes. However you approach them, expect students to treat the discussion as significant and highly charged, so be careful not to interpret understandable signs of nervousness as indicative of their possible guilt.

How much evidence is enough?

Confirming a case of student plagiarism is an academic judgement made within the requirements of civil law. Whereas criminal law requires proof beyond reasonable doubt, civil law is based on the balance of probabilities. Plagiarism cases cannot be managed under criminal law because plagiarism is not illegal, although there are rare occasions when students breach the regulation covering submission of material, and do so via theft or menacing threats, which are illegal. So, when considering how much evidence is needed to confirm a case, the question becomes, 'Which way does the case tip: more likely that the work is the student's own or more likely that it is not?'

Most people collect more evidence than they need to tip the balance of probabilities. Some get caught up in the process ('It took me two days but I found the book she copied from'). Some falsely assume a case cannot be made without finding the original source for every single instance where copying occurred. Some feel they must construct a case that will withstand challenge, no matter how robust that case must be. This kind of over-proof is more likely where assessors feel they themselves are under threat, or where the institution wrongly uses legal analogies and terminology derived from criminal law. On the other hand, where institutions recognise that it is the student's responsibility to be able to show it is their own work and where institutions collect 'case law' examples to show that decisions are made within established procedures and customary practice, then the assessors usually feel confident in their judgements. The result is a significant decrease in the time spent assembling evidence. In my own institution, where expertise is developed in a few responsible specialists, where case law is recorded and where the responsibilities of the student are clear, people rarely spend more than an hour collecting evidence to confirm plagiarism building a case and usually do so much more quickly.

Harris (2001, pp. 83-4), notes 'Emotionally charged meetings need clear structure if they are to maintain orderliness and a sense of objectivity. The value of knowing the rules and having a plan cannot be over-estimated.' He also cautions, 'Remember you may be wrong' and reminds the reader, 'therefore treat all students with respect.'

An activity for establishing 'how much is enough?'

1. Create a pack of statements, one per slip, some like those in the list below, and others arising from your own experience. Note: this activity works best in a group where each person has an identical pack of slips. Creating packs in different colours will make it easy to reconstitute the packs after use.

2. Turn the pack of slips face down then build a 'case' by turning up statements one by one. Each new slip adds to the evidence on the preceding slip. Keep adding a slip until the case 'tips' from more likely to be the student's own work to more likely not to be so.

3. When you have sufficient evidence to tip the balance of probabilities (and this is commonly after no more than three or four slips), move the slips to one side and build another 'case'.

In time, especially when working with others, you will develop a sense of 'enough' evidence and notice the pieces of evidence that seem especially relevant or convincing.

- This student did not attend any except the first of the scheduled supervision meetings for his undergraduate Honours dissertation. The submitted work is marked as a high 'B'.

- Two passages in the work seem very familiar but you are not sure of the source.

- The assessor says, 'This student's work just doesn't feel right'.

- The work being assessed is FAR better than that usually produced by this student.

- The work includes a complex statistical analysis of the data which is far beyond what is usually expected of undergraduates.

- The whole document uses variable language: in some parts, smooth, grammatical and correctly punctuated; in some parts, choppy and badly punctuated.

- Some of the document reads as if written by a native English speaker, some reads as if written by a second-language speaker.

- You find four 'Americanisms' in the first four pages of a ten-page document. The student is Australian.

- Four of the works cited in the text do not appear in the bibliography.

- When you check the 'Properties' function in an electronically-submitted piece of work, you find the document was created in 2002 and submitted in 2005.

- Four advanced Google searches yield verbatim unattributed lifts from Websites totalling 400 words in a 3,500 word document. The rest of the text shows variable language.

- The student admits 'a bit of plagiarism' but insists the work 'is my own and I cited a lot'. When asked the meaning of 'cited', the student says 'copied'.

- The work has a mix of Harvard referencing and Chicago referencing.

- The student's MSc is based on the returns from 900 questionnaires over three months in her home (i.e. non-UK) country.

- When asked to do so, the student can produce neither drafts nor copies of relevant research/articles on which the work is based.

- The formatting varies throughout with two sections in justified text.

- The submitted work only addresses a small aspect of the question rather than the whole assessment task and takes a surprising and unexpected line on that small aspect.

- The work uses dated sources (i.e. most recent reference is three years old and most references are pre-1995).

- The student's Turnitin report is coloured blue in the class list. [Blue signifies no matches found.]

- The student's side-by-side Turnitin report shows verbatim, unattributed 'lifts' from three Websites totalling 27% of the submitted work.

I ask the student to read a page or two of the essay. If he or she reads like it is the first time they have encountered the words, that becomes part of my case for assuming it is not the student's own work. If I notice that the student has difficulty with technical or unusual words, I ask for definitions.

See Chapter 8 for a discussion of ways in which institutions might handle detection other than by asking individual lecturers to undertake the investigation.

A final word

People tend to have very firm beliefs about how much evidence is needed to confirm plagiarism or about the extent to which academic judgement can be challenged. Senior managers and legal advisors often opt for what seems like justified caution or over-estimate the risks in labelling students' work as plagiarised. It may take careful presentation of the evidence about risk and the requirements of civil law to alter such longstanding beliefs and established practices. Chapter 8 offers suggestions on how you could encourage your own colleagues and institutional decision-makers to take on board some of the points raised in this chapter.

Answers for exercise on page 81

When this exercise appeared, the answers below were also provided as clues that the work was probably not the student's own:

1. Change of language, especially in the first paragraph. An advanced Google search for 'aspects of a dynamic agro-environment' locates the original source.

2. A fake reference at the end of the first paragraph.

3. Americanisms in paragraph two, one using a term differently ('corn' to mean maize), one an expression uncommon in UK English ('gotten'), and one US spelling (surely the weakest clue, as who doesn't spell this ailment strangely?).

4. Format changes between justified and unjustified text.

5. Line spacing changes (and in other instances, look for different fonts, formatting in html, hyperlinks left in grey, etc.).

6. Two different referencing systems used for in-text citation.

7. Line finishes in mid-sentence. A clue rather like 4 and 5 arising from careless cut-and-paste construction.

8. 'PTO' inappropriate – such carelessness does happen!

Penalties and outcomes for confirmed cases

In this chapter, the focus is on decisions about individual students whose plagiarism has been confirmed. What should happen next? What criterion should be used to select an appropriate penalty or outcome? It begins with the call from many quarters for more consistency and fairness in dealing with confirmed cases than is presently the case in many institutions and considers why consistency and fairness are difficult to achieve. This chapter also suggests ways to inform students in general about actions taken against the minority who do not abide by academic regulations. This is an often overlooked aspect of a holistic approach yet students report that one of their strongest deterrents is fear of being caught and of what might happen if they are (Lambert et al, 2006). In general, students rarely know what has happened to their peers except via the informal grapevine.

Suggestions made in this chapter sit alongside those in Chapter 8 covering broader issues of policy and procedure (plus, of course, actions described elsewhere as part of a holistic approach). Here, the goal is to ensure students are dealt with fairly, consistently and in accordance with the principles of natural justice once plagiarism has been detected, investigated and confirmed as described in Chapter 6 .

Setting a standard for managing cases

Both the popular and academic press often feature stories about what should or should not happen once plagiarism is confirmed. For example, Park's extensive review of students' experience of plagiarism in 2003 found an urgent need for 'penalty systems that are transparent and applied consistently' (p. 484). He implies, therefore, that most are neither, though a year later he describes how the University of Lancaster deals with cases to achieve these ends (Park, 2004). Two years on, in 2006, the leader writer for the *Times Higher Education Supplement* makes the same point, albeit with more sweeping language. Under the headline 'A Web of confusion' and after referral to 'horror stories' and 'indefensible inconsistencies' in how cases are managed, the leader writer concludes: '...staff do not know how to deal with it and universities do not know how to punish the perpetrators' (*THES*, 23 June 2006). The concerns are not UK-specific. Three New Zealand academics surveyed two tertiary institutions and were not impressed with penalties which seemed to have little or no impact on students' behaviour or '…academic progress in the medium or long term. Indeed some students may consider such risks to be part of the standard management of a tertiary learning career' (Lambert et al, 2006, p. 500).

Official organisations responsible for universities' quality assurance make similar statements. In 2004, the annual report of the UK Office of Independent Adjudicators (OIA) called for more consistency and, two years later, its head reiterated the point in a conference (where she made the statements included in the next few sentences). In all but one OIA case, students accepted that they had plagiarised but were not willing to accept the punishments as fair or the procedures as correctly followed. The OIA head herself noted 'too great a range of penalties to be defensible and many cases [that] would not stand up to legal scrutiny'. She quoted complainants who asked, 'Why have I been thrown out while my friend in a different department who did the same thing is not?'. She said, 'I am worried by the harshness of some of the penalties' then cited a case where a student who plagiarised 12 words in a long dissertation was denied not only a degree but any academic credit for three years' work (though the case, she said, was withdrawn and the decision altered in ways she did not describe). Her demand? 'It cannot be impossible for the sector to come together and share levels of punishment' (Deech, 2006).

Voices naming punishment as too harsh are matched by those claiming they are too lenient. They call for the opposite – stronger penalties to ensure academic standards are not threatened and that students are not 'getting away with it'.

The response from many universities and colleges, given the level of criticism and popular press coverage, has been relatively slow in coming. In 2005, a colleague and I surveyed nine UK colleges and universities, asking how their current management compared to that of five years previously. All said that changes were underway, prompted by concerns about current case management, especially consistency, but few had managed to move beyond the first few stages of their plans. In common with most universities and colleges, they knew they would struggle to defend or even explain their current treatment of some of their students.

Students who admitted engaging in any form of academic dishonesty reported that the most common reason they did so was because they were unlikely to be caught. …. As one student respondent said, when asked to comment on the topic of academic dishonesty within his institution, 'Welcome to Paradise'.

Lambert et al (2006, p. 449)

Think about:

- how consistent is punishment in your institution?

- if you wished to adopt a system of shared tariffs to increase institutional consistency, where might you start?

- how could you inform students of this change?

Inconsistency in punishment decisions

I have never met anyone concerned with plagiarism who wished to be inconsistent or unfair to students. However, well-meaning practices can deliver outcomes which are both. To demonstrate this in workshops, I often ask participants to consider three cases which have been confirmed as plagiarism and where they can assume authority to use all the penalties on a list I provide. Their task is to decide individually which penalty or combination of penalties is most appropriate for each student. As an aside, the penalty list derives from one university's actual practice in 2001; it is not an exemplar of good practice.

I have tried this task with over 1,000 people during four years in four countries and the results are almost always the same. Participants do the task then seem genuinely surprised to discover that others have come to different – sometimes markedly different – conclusions. When presented with the results from previous attempts by a different group, they are equally surprised to see that differences between groups were often greater than those within the group doing the exercise. Two typical responses are shown here.

Case 1: A final-year nursing student submitted a 3,000-word piece of coursework 75% of which was a verbatim copy from a Website without in-text acknowledgement of the source or the words themselves. The site was not listed under 'Bibliography'. When interviewed, she defended the practice by saying this is what she had done for the last three years and no one else had said it is unacceptable.

Case 2: Student A and Student B are studying Biology in Year 2 of a 3-year programme. Student A entered the programme in Year 2 from Hong Kong and missed the compulsory skills module in Year 1. Student B is British. The two students submit individual lab reports that show a 60% overlap of text with identical conclusions, spelling mistakes and data. Both strongly deny copying.

Plagiarism is not adequately addressed in my department. The tendency is to…only punish those with a blatant disregard for academic honesty, and even then, the punishment does not adequately fit the crime. A complicating factor is cultural difference. I tended to treat all students as equals and hold them all to the stated standard. However, I think that this [cultural difference] often clouds departments' judgement.

Comments by Canadian Teaching Assistants
http://www.sfu.ca/ integritytaskforce/ TAComments.htm

Case 3: A mature-entry student (previous 12 years spent working as a chef) submits an essay at the beginning of the second term with highly variable language – some fluent, some choppy and ungrammatical. There is no in-text citation.

Decisions in one group of 22 people (• indicating one person's choice)

Action recommended	Case 1	Case 2A	Case 2B	Case 3
1. discussion with teacher, no record				• • • •
2. discussion with a specialist officer, no record	•	•	•	• • • • •
3. student corrects work, full marks	•	• •	• •	• • • • •
4. student resubmits new work, full marks	• •	• • •	• • •	• •
5. marker disregards plagiarised work, grades the rest		•	•	• • • • •
6. student submits new work for a reduced mark	• • • • •	• • • • •	• • • • •	
7. student resubmits corrected work for capped pass	• • • • •	• •	• • •	
8. marker awards 0 for the work	•	• •	• •	
9. marker awards 0 for the module	• • •	• •		
10. university reduces final award (e.g. DipHE instead of BA)	• •			
11. removal from the programme				
12. removal from the university	• •			

Decisions in one group of 19 people (• indicating one person's choice)

Action recommended	Case 1	Case 2A	Case 2B	Case 3
1. discussion with teacher, no record				•
2. discussion with a specialist officer, no record	•	•	•	•
3. student corrects work, full marks			••	••••••
4. student resubmits new work, full marks		••	•	•••
5. marker disregards plagiarised work, grades the rest		•	••	
6. student submits new work for a reduced mark	••	•••••	••••	••
7. student resubmits corrected work for capped pass	••••	•••	•••	••••
8. marker awards 0 for the work	••••• •••	•••••	••••••	•
9. marker awards 0 for the module	•	•	•	
10. university reduces final award (e.g. DipHE instead of BA)				
11. removal from the programme	•			
12. removal from the university	•			

Looking at these two examples (and bearing in mind that the student does not get the average, but just one of these choices), one participant would reward the actions of the nursing student in case one with an extension and a chance to try again, and several would remove him or her from the university.

Honour codes and cheating

In 2001, a University of Virginia physics professor developed a tool for checking 1,800 pieces of his students' work and found 158 who seemed to have copied ('virtual replicas'). All faced expulsion as this was the only penalty allowed under the institution's honour code. The story made headlines around the world, triggered much discussion about the place of honour codes in the 21st century, and created work for administrators and lawyers. Simon et al (2004) describe lawsuits against the university and claims of racial bias in determining guilt. Eighteen months later, *The Cavalier Daily* (26 November 2002) reported the outcome of the 59 cases that went to an 'honour trial'. 48 left the university (c. 2% of the original cohort) and the Chair said, 'The system passed the test'. Another described the work involved as 'a massive load that came as a shock to the system'.

(Note: the Web page where I found this news article contained three paid advertisements, two of which offered to write essays for students.)

The case for individual decisions

Some argue that letting those close to students decide a penalty means students receive bespoke, nuanced consequences for plagiarism. However, the costs probably exceed the benefit and are not limited to observers of university practice such as the OIA and QAA. Inconsistency aggravates students and inhibits their willingness to engage with academic regulations which they perceive as 'unfair' and 'a lottery' (Seymour 2006). Why try to follow the rules when things happen (or do not happen) at the whim of the institution or a particular marker? Larkham and Manns (2002) found that students' reactions to inconsistent treatment matched those caught by a speed camera – the ones who are detected and punished see themselves as 'unlucky' and 'victimised' (p. 347).

Before proposing a way to deliver consistent penalties, it is worth briefly reviewing a strategy at the opposite end of the spectrum. Some institutions and indeed, whole national systems, award the same penalty for all cases, regardless of the circumstances. I have visited departments where any plagiarism attracts a zero for the work. Some American universities operate a strict honour code where students pledge at enrolment to abide by all the rules. Any breach, however minor, results in immediate expulsion. In Sweden, all cases that are referred to formal disciplinary panels can only be awarded a suspension of university attendance for a shorter or longer period of time with the right of return, or a letter of warning then no further action.

One-size-fits-all approaches suffer from the fact that they never actually do. As anyone who has dealt with more than a few cases will attest, each instance of plagiarism involves a range of factors and mitigating circumstances. This approach, closer to conformist than consistent, is probably unacceptable in the UK under human rights legislation. Unless it is also used with great care and other supporting activities (McCabe, 2003) it is counter-productive in that it blocks students' emerging sense of how academics defend and define their values. Having only one or two penalties also makes academics I meet very reluctant to report cases because in most circumstances, 'their' students would be treated too harshly or too leniently. Instead, they bypass systems completely. This tendency (along with a concern about time and lack of confidence that the case could be substantiated) probably accounts for the difference between students who say they were caught (5.8% of respondents in one survey reported by Lambert et al, 2006) and those officially recognised as going through university procedures (0.2% in the same survey).

The case for fairness

A group of researchers in Nevada, USA (Simon et al, 2003 and 2004) demonstrated what many would see as self-evident: students and academics choose whether or not to use policies and procedures and are unwilling to do so with those they see as unfair.

Universities can be assumed to react in a similar way and to build in procedures that underpin the goal of fairness. They do so if they:

- require that a student be presented with all the evidence;

- give the student an opportunity to challenge the evidence in front of the person or body that will determine the punishment;

- provide all participants in the process with appropriate notice;

- offer students information on their rights including representation by 'an appropriately skilled and qualified person, particularly in serious or complex cases' (Carroll and Appleton, 2001);

- advise students on how evidence can be challenged;

- impose penalties that are proportionate to the magnitude of the offence.

This last point is probably the most difficult to achieve because of the complex circumstances in many (some would even say most)

[A student commented that] receiving a warning in the first year for relying too heavily on set text material from the tutor acted to legitimise the use of his [the student's] own personal voice. Through the warning he not only went away to learn how to reference properly so he would not get 'caught out' again but also came to a better understanding of how to use secondary sources and be original in the way of looking at them. [The student] concluded by saying that he now not only gets better marks but finds that the tutors appreciate the value of his work, too.

Freewood (2001, p.4)

plagiarism cases. Another factor is that individual academics' views on proportionality differ. All of the thousands of academics I have encountered in my work in this field have been clear in their commitment to fair treatment for their own students (though of course, with the occasional cynical comment thrown in). In general, all agree natural justice must apply. But they define that differently, as the workshop exercise on pages 92–93 demonstrates.

Some findings on who reports cases at an American university

'Faculty who are more confident in the university as an institution are more likely to employ formal administrative methods…and more likely to exercise the full range of options open to them.'

'Faculty members who are "Sceptical" appear to eschew administrative processes and deal with cases in a more private manner, often involving bargaining.'

'[F]ormalizing academic dishonesty cases opens faculty members to the scrutiny of others and may contribute – rightly or wrongly – to the view that the latter are less capable and less effective as instructors. Further research will be necessary to support this conjecture.'

'[F]emale faculty are significantly more likely to be "Sceptical" of the institution than are male faculty—regardless of academic rank.'

Simon et al (2003)

First, create a framework

Initial attempts to set consistent, proportionate penalties resulted in taxonomies of offences derived from past cases. One paper by Walker (1998) was frequently cited by subsequent authors, including myself, since it addressed for almost the first time what actually happens when students are penalised. Walker listed eight varieties of plagiarism ranging from 'sham paraphrasing' at the lowest end to 'purloining' as the most serious offence, all encountered in his own institution in New Zealand. He then created a table where punishments for minor and major examples of each sort were stated in general terms so that, for example, 'minor illicit paraphrasing' had 'marks deducted equal to 10-50% of the assigned value, depending on amount, no resubmission permitted'. Four years later, Larkham and Manns (2002) did the same exercise with four UK cases. They created small case studies describing the circumstances, noted the penalties for each one, and outlined some of the thinking that lay behind the final decision(s).

Taxonomies and case studies serve as a marker for judging others' practice but are never detailed or numerous enough to become case law or to guide future actions. They cannot deliver consensus as called for by the head of the OIA locally, let alone at a national level. That requires a generic framework, adopted in principle by all institutions, but able to manifest itself differently in line with local circumstances. Such a framework would use weighted criteria for making decisions and a step-by-step process for arriving at conclusions. Where frameworks are in use (and I have seen instances in more than a dozen examples in UK higher education), the result is a transparent and defensible system able to withstand challenge, should any arise. More importantly, using a framework can improve consistency because it permits monitoring and evaluation as described in Chapter 8. Institutions who take this approach are already sharing and reviewing each others' actions via publications, conference presentations and role-specific gatherings such as meetings of university Registrars. When and if more do so, a national consensus should emerge.

While universities wait for the consensus (and that is likely to be a long wait), they need to remind their often vociferous critics that complex issues such as student plagiarism managed in complex organisations such as universities will not be resolved overnight. Consistency is something towards which we strive, and I guess that the critics will be reassured by evidence that action is underway.

Necessary steps in an 'actuarial' approach

An 'actuarial' approach is one where criteria and process are set up in advance of actual decisions then applied to an individual case. Institutions that have worked steadily towards an 'actuarial approach' usually do these things:

1   Begin their dealing with a student by establishing the level of breach of academic regulations.

2   Agree in advance the factors that will be considered when matching a penalty to the level of breach (often called 'the tariff' where specific levels of breach match with a small range of potential outcomes or penalties).

3   Record all decisions and hold a central record that can be accessed by other decision-makers.

4   Regularly monitor and review the recorded data for consistency; intervene where and if it falls below an acceptable level.

Each of these will now be considered in more detail.

Establishing the level of breach

Although it is difficult to define and even trickier sometimes to gain a common understanding of plagiarism as outlined in Chapter 1, university policies almost always use unequivocal language: you commit a breach of academic regulations if you pass off others' work as your own. Some breaches are more serious than others. I think talk of breaches being serious is more useful than the more commonly encountered 'minor plagiarism' and 'major plagiarism' labels you find in many policy documents. It's the *breach* that is minor or major, not the plagiarism. Plagiarism, like pregnancy, is an absolute condition but the consequences will vary widely depending on the student's individual context and sometimes, on mitigating circumstances, and all these will contribute to the judgement as to how seriously the student has not complied with regulations.

To deal fairly and consistently with this variation in consequences, institutions first need to classify levels of breach and use a range of strategies to do so. I met a department head in one UK university who drew on his work as a magistrate to create a form where aggravating and mitigating factors are laid out in two columns and the table is then used that to make a judgement on the best penalty in a particular case. Another institution classifies severity according to the number of times the student has committed an offence (see Park, 2004 and table below). An 'actuarial' approach is adopted by Yeo and Chien (2005) from Curtin University. They select four criteria then score each one for the case in question on a scale of 1 (designating a low level) to 9 (for the most serious). Once all four are scored, the 'profile' points to one of three levels (helpfully called I, II and III). A 2005 study which the authors did to evaluate the Curtin system using case study material showed, '…staff *can* [original emphasis] use the four criteria in a consistent manner [although] the decision on overall level for a given case is possibly influenced by:

- an implicit weighting given to one criterion

- their confidence in making decisions using the criteria; or

- on a number of factors outside these [four].'

The authors concluded that staff seemed least confident in making judgements about students' intentions and tended to be more conservative overall in their judgements when any one factor was very low.

Criteria and range

Criteria used by Curtin University to establish the seriousness of cases:

1 **experience** of the student [ranges from new or inexperienced students through to those nearing completion of their course or thesis]

2 **nature** of the plagiarism [ranges from poor paraphrasing, citation and referencing skills through to wholesale copying or appropriation of others' work] citing Park, 2004 and Walker, 1998

3 **extent** or amount of work that is plagiarised [ranges from a few elements with little impact on overall assessment to a significant proportion defined as more than 10% and/or having the effect of significantly compromising the assessment]

4 **intention** of the student to plagiarise or to cheat by way of plagiarism [ranges from unintentional or careless acts through to deliberate intent to commit fraud]

Another example of the criteria-based approach

This version has been in use for six years at the time of writing at my own institution, Oxford Brookes University. Our approach resembles that found at Curtin, although the criteria and procedures differ. In our case, specialist officers are the only people authorised to deal with cases and their responsibility (once they have confirmed the case) is to decide between three levels of breach, defined as *negligent academic practice, academic malpractice* and *academic misconduct*. The procedures stipulate the decision on level must derive from only four factors, ranked to reflect each criterion's weighting. The criteria are:

1 **extent** of the plagiarism including where in the piece of work it occurs. This means, for example, that the same amount of copying in a methodology section of a dissertation or in the appendices would probably be viewed as less serious than the same amount in the conclusion section;

2 **level** of the student's progress in their academic 'career' with special attention paid to students who enter with credit in Years Two and Three;

99

3   **presumed knowledge** of the student of the academic regulations. This is based on evidence rather than the student's assertion and takes into account any overt teaching, skills development or information. The student's stated intention may be one of the pieces of evidence used to make this judgement though this presents problems as discussed in more detail on page 104;

4   **rules of the discipline.** Students will have been given a range of rules and requirements when studying in different fields and the underpinning assumptions about, for example, the role of a citation or the type of writing students are expected to master. Schott (2003) explored the various roles of the reference in a two-page article for the Royal Society of Medicine, itself containing 30 references, ' …in certain genres of writing – the recording of anecdotes, narratives, and even hunches – the lack of citations is no drawback and is even admissable' (p. 191 where the original of this sentence contained three footnotes).

Using the above criteria and following the rules for weighting would mean that how serious one considered the breach of a particular student would have more to do with how much of the submitted work had not been correctly attributed than with the level of the student's study. For example, a student in term one of Year one who submitted work that was 80% copied verbatim from the Web could not be classified as negligent, the lowest level of breach. Nor could the student be managed by reducing the overall grade and offering feedback on citation because a breach had occurred. In this example, a more appropriate classification would be *academic malpractice,* but this would need checking with reference to the third criterion to be sure that the more serious *academic misconduct* was not warranted. If, when investigating the student's knowledge of the regulations and whether or not he has gained the skill to comply in the short time since enrolment, the student shows little or no ability to do what was expected, then raising the level is unwarranted. This is a case of *malpractice.*

Selecting a penalty from a list

Think about:

* what punishments are applied in your own university?
  In your school or department? For your own students?

* how were they determined and by whom?

* are they widely known or public?

Where markers are free to select any penalty (as was the case in my own institution in 1999), some become inventive ('You two copied and the work is worth 60%. You can each have 30%, now go away'). Others inadvertently benefit colluders by giving them an extension: ('You two copied. Go away and do it again using this new data and this time, work alone'). And a few who are left to their own devices make links that are probably unjustified: ('You two copied. This is a serious breach of what we expect from professional nurses and reflects on your capacity for ethical practice. Go and see the university discipline panel').

Specifying penalties means universities can track and monitor decisions, encourage consensus and protect students from over-zealous or over-imaginative treatment. A penalty list must be broad enough to allow for a range of circumstances and narrow and specific enough to ensure they can be monitored. The example below operates in the University of Lancaster in the UK and was published in a detailed paper describing what the author calls 'an institutional framework for dealing with plagiarism' (Park, 2004).

Number of offences	Range of penalties
First offence	• Warning the student • Asking the marker to 'set aside sections involving plagiarised text' • Student repeats and resubmits the work for a minimum pass • Awarding a zero if the student refuses or does not resubmit
Second offence	• Awarding a zero for the work; no reassessment • Student advised of consequences of any other further offence • Record kept on student's file
Third or fourth offence	• Referral to the Standing Academic Committee • Recommendation for permanent exclusion from the University

Penalties available to the Standing Academic Committee for a third offence	• to permit the student to repeat the work for a minimal pass mark
	• to award 0 for the work
	• to award 0 for all coursework or dissertation
	• to award 0 for the unit or module
	• where 0 for the unit or module has no impact on the degree classification, to recommend a final award one class below that calculated from the student's record
	• to exclude the student permanently from the University or, if the offence is detected after the final assessment, not to award the degree

Park, C. (2004), 'Rebels without a clause: towards an institutional framework for dealing with plagiarism by students', *Journal of Further and Higher Education* 28:3, p. 297

Linking the level with the penalty

Many universities follow the example of the University of Lancaster and link the level and the penalty – in my own institution, we refer to this connection as a tariff. Only specialist officers called Academic Conduct Officers (ACOs) can designate levels. ACOs also have delegated authority to award five penalties, or to refer cases involving a breach severe enough to warrant a punishment above a 0 grade from the module leader to a university disciplinary committee where a wide range of options are available. The shading in the table opposite shows how Oxford Brookes University matches the level of breach with designated penalties.

To illustrate how ACOs use the tariff, the case of the student whose breach was designated as academic malpractice in the previous example on page 100 illustrates the conundrums that remain, even with a tariff framework. In order to establish the level, the student will already have been interviewed by the ACO, told of the breach, advised on where to seek future help and informed how this will be recorded. Many argue that these are already penalties enough. However, since this is malpractice rather than negligence, the tariff stipulates that another penalty is warranted. The choice is between penalty 2 (removing the copied material and marking the rest) or penalty 3 (suggesting a reduction in marks). At this point, case law comes into play as well as referral back to the original four criteria.

Choosing penalty 2 in a case of such extensive plagiarism would mean the student was awarded a few marks at best. Is this proportionate?

Penalty tariffs recommended for three different levels of breach

Penalty (in brief)	Negligent Academic Practice	Academic Malpractice	Academic Misconduct
1. A recorded conversation with an ACO + warning of future breaches			
2. Marker disregards the breach(es) + marks the rest of the work to arrive at a grade			
3. Reduction in marks by stated amount; resubmission of corrected work for a capped mark or capped pass			
4. 0% for the piece of work			
5. 0% for the module or course			
6. Referral of the student to University Disciplinary Committee			

On the other hand, penalty 3 would entail advising the marker to reduce the grade by a stated small amount (usually about 10%) and to mark the actual work the student did to create the piece. Assessed work might include searching for sources, organising the work, writing the conclusion or whatever the assessment criteria specifies. A marker where academic malpractice is confirmed may treat unattributed material as if it were the student's own for the purpose of arriving at a grade and mark. However, with such extensive verbatim copying (in this example, an 80% verbatim 'lift' from the Web without attribution), the assessor would probably struggle to judge whether the student had met the learning outcomes. Did the student understand the text? Without any transformation of the original material, it is probably impossible to tell. Penalty 3, therefore, like penalty 2 is likely to result in a very low mark since in a sense the student loses twice – once through inability to meet the learning outcomes due to plagiarism and once as a result of the reduction. ACOs at Oxford Brookes University have spent considerable time and effort discussing how to deal with this fairly.

As the sample shows, a 10% reduction can seem a relatively small penalty but might mean the student fails the module, either for the reasons already given or because the reduction takes them below the 'pass' threshold. Not to award a penalty because of the risk of failure is explicitly precluded; it would take other criteria into account. We do, however, require a fairness check to ensure the impact on the student is not disproportionate. (There is a more detailed discussion of mitigation in later sections.)

The tariff required four years of discussion (and other institutions doing something similar report equally protracted activity). However, this turned out to be necessary. It created the consensus needed for consistency, and continued to be necessary in the two years following the application of the tariff to all cases. Indeed, when energy flagged or when meetings became scarce and induction was less than satisfactory, the ACOs' consistency when using the tariff fell, too. (See Carroll and Seymour (2006) for more discussion of the importance of developing a community of practice in order to enhance consistency and how actual practice is not always as tidy as stated procedures.) Academic Conduct Officers at Oxford Brookes University found that publishing the tariff made their decisions transparent but also conferred other benefits. Discussing the tariff with students during interviews helped students understand their own actions and see more clearly what they must do in future.

Difficulties with considering intention

Students often assert their plagiarism was unintentional and that they were unaware of their responsibilities concerning citation and attribution. Many do so with great feeling. On the other hand, I know of students who admit intent when none was present because unless they do, their penalties could not be decided by their teacher or department. If they denied it or showed lack of contrition, the case could not be 'minor' and must go through the full disciplinary procedure. In my view, this smacks of coercion and students involved could well end up amongst those complaining to the Office of Independent Adjudicators.

Whether students deny or own up to intentional plagiarism, what matters is the academic judgement about whether, on balance, the claim is likely to be correct. Specialists in my own institution who deal with dozens or even hundreds of cases every year and who often discuss this issue when they meet to review cases have learned to look out for these signs:

- **Are there deliberate attempts to conceal?** One example might be a student who references carefully in some parts of the paper then provides no in-text citation in a section that shows extensive copying. One ACO said it is unlikely to be naivety that drives a student to use the 'find and replace' function to change the name of the product being reviewed whereas the opposite is probably true of a student who includes the name of a free essay bank in his bibliography (although a cynic is likely to point out that in the latter, other explanations may also apply).

- **Has the student any 'previous form'?** A record of a warning issued at an earlier meeting significantly lessens the probability of confusion. Care is needed because a previous warning for copying in group work submissions may not necessarily transfer to an understanding about the requirements of, say, in-text citation.

- **Has the student received specific instruction or had opportunities to learn the rules?** A student who passed a compulsory study skills module that included instruction on correct use of internet material has been alerted to her responsibilities. The same can also be said for the student interviewed by a colleague who, at the point of submission for a PhD, claimed to be unaware of the need to cite others' ideas.

- **Is the extent so large that no reasonable person would see the action as academically appropriate?** For example, a new international student who comes from a culture where ways of demonstrating your knowledge differ from those in the UK can nevertheless be assumed to know that a 100% copy of a 3,000 word essay written by a cousin does not match the instruction in the assessment brief to 'use your own words'. On the other hand, the same student constructing a paper by patching together others' words drawn from a range of carefully chosen sources without citation marks could still be using old rules to play this new UK 'game'. The result is plagiarism and should not be overlooked as that does not help the student learn. Rather it should be dealt with in accordance with the suggestions in this chapter, assuming in the second example that the student was not intent on deception and at most labelling her actions as negligent. The first example is probably misconduct.

A UK computing lecturer describes his second lecture to final year students preparing for their final year project:

I cover anonymised details of the incidents from the preceding year. This includes the overall extent of non-original work, the number of projects that were investigated in depth, the number of cases that went to formal inquiry stage and the number and extent of the penalties that were imposed. The lecture concludes with a plea that the following year, I will have no incidents to report, no students with their classification reduced, none who were delayed by a year and none who were denied an award.

- **How different was the student's previous academic setting to the current UK academic culture?** Students need time to set aside practices and assumptions that have previously served them well (such as some A-level practice that rewards quoting verbatim from texts without attribution) or to learn new skills (such as an office worker who has never referenced work before embarking on degree-level study). While such students are making the transition, assumptions about intention need to take the 'distance travelled' into account.

Not intending plagiarism does not exonerate the student – plagiarism is plagiarism. But the converse, i.e. clearly intending to create a false impression in the assessor as to whose work is being judged, might be grounds for awarding an increased punishment. So, too, would other compounding offences such as extracting work with menaces, lying about the source of data, stealing others' work, or using someone else's work despite the original owner's stipulation that this should not occur. (Proving the last point can be difficult but we did have one case where a student set up covert video surveillance in his flat and submitted the tape as evidence that flatmates who copied his work broke the lock to his room. He was found to have taken sufficient steps to protect the work and was recommended to change accommodation.)

Dealing with mitigation

There are two ways to look at mitigation. Most academics regard students who say they cut corners or broke the rules because of their part-time work or because three pieces of work were due in that week as engaging in justification rather than explanation. These are largely ignored. Sometimes, students explain or justify their actions because of things such as illness, family bereavement or personal stress. These cannot be mitigation for breaching regulations because mechanisms are already in place to deal with them. Students are usually informed early in their studies about seeking an extension or additional help and can reasonably be expected to follow designated channels.

Other issues linked to mitigation are more problematic. Fairness dictates that the overall outcome should not be disproportionate to the offence, yet the same decision may delay one student's progression for 12 months and only result in a lower mark for another in the same programme. This could happen, for instance, if a 10% reduction in marks pushed the first student below a pass in a compulsory module that was only taught in one semester and was a prerequisite for others. A more significant impact might be the consequences of a charge of misconduct on a student's future professional status. Students who are guilty of not abiding by academic conventions by, for example, misusing the finer points of citation have plagiarised but so have those who commission ghost writers or fellow students to write their coursework for them. The former offence is probably only significant within academia, whereas the latter is universally seen as deliberate cheating and by many, it is seen as fraud. If your institution does not make such distinctions, you will need to seek advice before allocating punishments that evoke a full disciplinary process for all plagiarism. It would not be just to deny someone the right to be a nurse, a social worker or to practise law, for example, because of a minor violation of referencing conventions which automatically becomes a charge of misconduct. Whether or not it would be just to do so in the case of more serious or even fraudulent acts is more controversial. So far, I have not been able to find evidence of a link between what students do as students and what professionals do, for example when administering drugs. Students in survey after survey are clear that the two decisions differ and their attitudes towards them differ, too. One of the more provocative findings concerns Canadian pharmacy students who conformed to all the behaviours found in other surveys, as did their teachers. The study argued that breaking the rules was a necessary step in students' 'moral evaluation' and that 'moral development must be preceeded by the opportunity to act immorally' (Austin et al, 2005, p. 155). The authors note that dealing with consequences is central to fully developed moral reasoning skills.

Deciding whether mitigation is justified because of the link between the penalty and the student's future academic career is not straightforward. Most decision makers I have talked to say that students who know what is expected, have the skills to comply, and who are aware of the consequences should they not do so are acting as informed adults. Students can be expected, therefore, to take the consequences that flow from their actions. After long thought, I agree, though note that often only one or two of these conditions apply. You will need to reach your own conclusion on these difficult matters and must ensure you act consistently with colleagues and your institution's stated procedures. Again, this is an issue that is regularly discussed when Oxford Brookes University ACOs meet and which the more sweeping statements made by critics at the beginning of this chapter fail to take into account when they pronounce about consistency as if attaining it were a straightforward matter.

Publicising punishment decisions

Punishments can be used to inform and teach an individual student but will only be effective for students as a whole if disciplinary actions are made public without, of course, reverting to 'name and shame' tactics. Publication could also counter the more fanciful messages that circulate on the informal grapevine when measures to tackle plagiarism are introduced. Your own institution will probably offer several channels such as student representatives, a regular column in the student newspaper, or specific mention at induction sessions. Wherever you give the message, take care to balance it with measures that involve students and value their learning. Without that balance, students might over-react, assuming perhaps that you are running a 'catch and punish' programme or, if numbers are small, that statistics imply permission to transgress with impunity.

Plagiarism cases are not publicized, so I don't know how often it happens. I think it warrants a mention at the beginning of the class, but a reminder before every paper is a bit much. If a professor catches someone, say in another class, I would like to know. If I were harboring any thoughts of cheating, this would let me know that my professor is on top of these things, and cheating doesn't pay.

Contributor to a US discussion board under the question, 'Do professors worry too much about plagiarism?'

Institutional policy and culture

8

Much of this Handbook concentrates on individuals' actions and responsibilities. Here, the focus is on frameworks and procedures that support and resource case management. In the five years since the first edition of the Handbook, examples of effective practice have emerged and some have been published. Examples include the description of changes at the University of Lancaster (Park, 2004) and Price's frequently quoted 2002 article 'Beyond Gotcha' about American universities. In Australia, many universities have taken a strategic approach such as Flinders University's Academic Integrity Management Strategy. This chapter is largely aimed at those who have not yet started to rethink their policies and procedures and draws on the literature and on my own travels to a large number of places around the world to see their practices at first hand. If you or your institution is already well down the road to revising how you manage cases, you might find referring to others' approaches interesting or, more usefully, publish your own to add to the resources that will help the whole HE community become more effective.

> **Think about:**
>
> - do staff use the policy? Do they trust it to treat them and their students fairly?
>
> - if staff bypass current policies and offer 'rough justice' instead, why might that happen?

Why review is necessary

As a rule of thumb, policies and procedures for dealing with plagiarism that have not been reviewed, evaluated and updated in the last few years are probably not fit for purpose. In almost all tertiary institutions, plagiarism is now an everyday occurrence rather than the unwelcome surprise it was in the 1980s and 1990s when most policies were written. Back then, policies assumed all plagiarism happened because of a deliberate effort to cheat, yet now we also recognise students' misunderstanding and misuse of regulations as well as their misconduct. The result of 21st century realities is a large and growing number of cases that must be handled quickly and efficiently. In my own university, we have seen a 100% increase on the previous year's total, year on year, for the last six years, with no sign that this trend is changing. Others report similar increases.

Although the need for a rethink is generally acknowledged, it may not trigger action because it has to compete with so many other demands for resources and staff time. Most tertiary institutions will be coping with a steep rise in recruitment of students *per se* and the students they recruit will be more diverse than ever, including a growing number of international students. Senior managers must attend to quality assurance, income generation, research standing and student-centred delivery, all of which, in turn, usually end up on teachers' shoulders as well. Increases in staff workload are regularly documented. The list could go on (and often does when staff find the time to meet and chew over such matters). A review of policies for dealing with plagiarism must find a way to sit within this challenging context. One important first step is to show how, in fact, dealing with plagiarism links to and is essential in delivering all these other key priorities.

Need for review?

An institution probably needs to review their current policies and procedures if any of these signs are present:

- No clearly documented evidence of where students are taught the skills necessary to comply with academic regulations and the conventions of academic writing.

- The absence of clear approaches to ensure that students are aware of academic regulations and the need to uphold academic integrity and what their responsibilities are in complying with these.

- No clear evidence that the university promotes academic integrity as a primary value for staff and students ('…Contrary evidence would need to go beyond rhetoric, mission statements and general admonitions' p. 242).

- A lack of staff development activities relevant to deterring plagiarism to ensure all staff are familiar with current procedures and regulations, good practice in course design, approaches to detection and any legal responsibilities.

- Evidence that staff may be taking individual decisions that could lead to inconsistent or unfair treatment.

- No systematic approach to collecting the data on the occurrence of cases of plagiarism (both intentional and unintentional.

- Statistics that reveal the detection of a small number of cases. By 'small' we mean a number that is significantly lower than that which statistics suggest are likely to occur. The 'rule of thumb' of 10% may or may not be helpful in specific cases but could be a useful starter for enquiry as to whether the number of detected cases is significantly below this figure.

Macdonald and Carroll, 2006

- **Remit.** Is the group to collect data and make recommendations or actually draft a policy? Will they create a final version after feedback and revision? Is the group being asked to provide guidance on underlying principles such as the balance of emphasis between academic integrity and valuing students' learning on the one hand and outlawing unacceptable behaviours and punishing offenders on the other? Some policies only address plagiarism whereas others include misconduct in exams and other breaches such as duplication, fabrication and deception of various kinds.

Seeking legal advice

Early information-gathering should include clarifying legal and procedural matters such as data protection, human rights legislation, copyright, and above all, the need to ensure procedures for assessment are completely separate from those for dealing with plagiarism. (For legal confirmation of this last point, see Nolan (1994) on *R v Manchester Metropolitan University*.) Once the separation from assessment is established, there may be a need to revise guidance to examination boards and external examiners. Both can continue to comment on assessment decisions in general and the means used to ensure they are fair, valid and reliable (including measures for dealing with plagiarism), but neither examination boards nor external examiners may revisit or seek to alter decisions, (including any about penalties). Decisions made under disciplinary procedures must stand. I regularly visit institutions where these matters are still blurred.

Many institutions also seek legal advice about the required level of proof for confirming cases. A few, even when the 'balance of probabilities' argument is made, continue to be unwilling to proceed without criminal levels of proof (i.e. beyond reasonable doubt). Some require that the source be found for any copying before a case is confirmed. Legal advice in both instances can help to reassure senior managers of appropriate levels of proof. My understanding is that academic judgements, made in accord with stated procedures, are not subject to legal challenge except on grounds of unfairness or vexation. No challenge is likely to be successful if the amount of evidence to support the case is sufficient to justify the academic judgement. Neither are they likely to be upheld if the amount of evidence outlined in Chapter 6 is offered. I understand that no successful challenge of such an academic judgement has happened in the world. People still fret about it but the reality appears to not support the concern. (As an aside, if you know to the contrary, I would be grateful for the information.)

The issues mentioned in this section do not constitute an exhaustive list. Legal advice is usually sought at some stage so it is useful to do so near the start of any review.

The case for using specialists

Most revised procedures that prove effective in practice are specifically designed around the difficulties of under-reporting and markers' reluctance to act when they suspect the work is not the student's own. Policies which seem to assume that detecting plagiarism, deciding to act, then following procedures exactly is automatic may indeed be able to affirm that procedures are in place, but are unlikely to be able to point to signals that they are effective.

The most common mechanism used to address under-reporting and failure to follow stated procedures is to separate the identification of a possible case from its subsequent confirmation and management. Instead of assuming the spotter will do both, 'plagiarism specialists' are appointed. Sometimes the specialist(s) is located in a central department, such as one responsible for examinations, quality assurance or linked to the academic registrar. Creating one or two central posts encourages maximum coherence, enhances consistency and usually results in speedy adoption.

There are disadvantages to centralising specialist roles as well. Although most teaching staff are quick to hand over cases, a few cling on to 'their' students, thus guaranteeing inconsistent treatment and often leaving students bewildered. The centralised model is reliant on the interpersonal skills and insider knowledge of the post holder(s). In places where I have seen this system working well, the person (or people) holds a role of a status sufficient to allow them to show their competence. On the other hand, I have visited places where people in such a role struggle to accommodate the disparate and often discipline-specific nature of plagiarism cases. It is common to hear those holding central responsibility say they are just managing their current caseload and even if the number is well below that which could be predicted, are reluctant to encourage steps that might increase the workload. More worryingly, it is common to meet centrally-placed specialists who have little or no idea about what students are taught or how assessments are set. In a way, this mirrors the way academics regard central specialists as being outside their area of concern. Both reactions mitigate against an effective and holistic approach. Finally, the job of centralised plagiarism specialist tends not to lend itself to overall job satisfaction. If, despite these drawbacks, your revised procedures opted for this model, you would need to find ways of addressing the issues listed above.

Another model involving specialists, which is used in a growing number of institutions, is to refer all cases to the head of department once a marker suspects plagiarism. This is usually the mechanism in revised policies on their first iteration, replacing, say, a 1980s version where all cases went to a full disciplinary board. There are two problems that are common with the 'refer to the Head' approach. In general, academics recognise that senior managers are already fully stretched by their workload and are reluctant to add more. Most managers I speak with find dealing with even a few cases, especially as they often occur together at peak times, makes planning ahead very difficult. Despite this, I have seen policies where the manager is potentially the recipient of cases from many thousands of students. The result is that academics bypass referral and when cases are referred, delays of months (and sometimes longer) are common, with some cases seeming to fizzle out rather than be resolved.

Some policies deal with concerns about workload by creating procedures for 'minor' and 'major' plagiarism with only the latter falling within institutional procedures. A quick trawl of policies produced these examples to explain the difference:

> The University of Edinburgh describes **poor scholarship** as work that is worthy of 'a poor mark and reveals a need for education'. The guidance notes give examples of cases where marks may be reduced:
>
>> inadequate citation of material (e.g. material copied from online sources without acknowledgement); marks for an element of submitted work may be shared between students who have clearly submitted joint work without acknowledgement where this is not allowed.

> The University of Liverpool defines **minor plagiarism** as:
>
>> a small amount of paraphrasing, quotation or use of diagrams, charts etc. without adequate citation. Minor plagiarism may result from poor scholarship (i.e. when a student, through inexperience or carelessness, fails to reference appropriately or adequately identify the source of the material which they use) or it may be a deliberate act but on a small scale.

Liverpool Hope University defines **major plagiarism** as:

> the inclusion of significant amounts of other people's
> work [e.g. large blocks of text, musical notation,
> program code, etc.] which clearly detracts from the
> originality of the student's work. This applies when
> there is no cited reference accompanying the copied
> content, even if the source is included in an
> accompanying bibliography; or if work is cited verbatim
> without the use of quotation markers (quotation marks
> or indenting).

Although each statement looks clear-cut in practice everyone who reads these policies will probably have a different understanding of their meaning and a different way of dealing with the mitigating and individual context of a specific student's actions. The 'minor you manage, major you refer' approach might deliver consistency in a very small and coherent unit where everyone knows the students and their colleagues well. Even then, transparency and defensibility would be strained. Outcomes that are not recorded, even if consistent, make it impossible to know what treatment or information an individual student has received. This approach to managing cases usually doesn't meet external requirements for fairness, consistency, and transparency in large, multi-faculty universities. When a revision of a 1990s policy opts for this approach, the result is a pretty quick rethink and often involves devolving responsibility to a different kind of specialist.

The model that I advocate (and that many are adopting) is one that identifies one or two staff who work in each subject area. Thus, a school of 40 or 50 academics might have one or two specialists charged with pursuing cases of plagiarism for a set number of hours per year alongside their other duties. This model ensures that cases are dealt with by someone who understands the academic area in question (and quite possibly knows the student as well). Limiting the numbers makes consistent decision-making a realistic possibility, maximises the cost benefits of any formal training provided and ensures expertise is maintained through regular practice. It is worth noting that, while the holder of such a role certainly needs a thorough understanding of the relevant academic issues, there is no automatic requirement that he or she be a member of the academic staff. He or she will, however, need to have this particular responsibility included in any workload planning or time allocation and will need to be supported by measures discussed below under institutional strategies.

When I describe this version of 'plagiarism specialist' to interested parties at workshops and institutional visits, the first thing people ask about is time. In my own institution where specialist officers called Academic Conduct Officers (ACOs) have been in place for six years at the time of writing, time allocation per ACO has stayed at about the same overall level that it was when the system began in 2000. The procedures assume two hours per case. However, in reality, the overall time requirement for each ACO has risen because the number of cases rises year on year. At the same time, the time requirement per case has fallen below the assumed two hours except for a few very complex ones. Questions of time and resources are therefore difficult to predict though several factors will help reduce time-per-case to manageable levels. They include:

- **Use of standard letters and pro formas** for communicating with students and recording decisions. This has the added benefit of more careful and accurate monitoring.

- **Consensus as to how much evidence is required.** Cases that are built to withstand challenges from elsewhere within the institution itself and/or from students and their lawyers will take large amounts of time. Those compiled where neither is permitted (as under our revised policy and procedures) take only enough time to tip the balance of probabilities (see Chapter 7). ACOs know they must reach a judgement that abides by the tariff and stays within 'case law' boundaries established through years of careful monitoring. Except in the occasional very complex case, they confirm and deal with a case in a fraction of the time cited by Larkham and Manns in 2002 where one case required 16 hours. They can do this, I think, because they meet regularly, share hints and tips and seek each others' advice.

- **Efficient interviewing skills**. ACO workloads are based on the assumption that all students are interviewed and that interviews last about an hour. Half the time is usually spent either confirming the case or deciding there is no breach of regulations. Students in confirmed cases have the choice of returning at another time with a supporter, something they are alerted to in the standard letter which also informs them they can bring a supporter for the confirmation interview. If the student agrees to continue (and only a tiny number over the years have not), the ACO then awards one of six designated penalties. The remaining 30 minutes are spent ensuring the student understands how their behaviour breached regulations and where to go for more support. The student is also told what needs to happen next and how, if they wish, they can appeal against the decision. A brief A4 form is completed and despatched to a central record and the case is finished.

A variation on the 'plagiarism specialist' model adopts most of the practices described for ACOs except that it uses small school-based panels, convened at stated times and able to manage all the cases that have arisen since the last panel meeting. Using small panels does require more resources than the ACO model, but yields the same benefits plus a few more. Panel decisions are more collegial and members can overtly share expertise. Students know when their case will be dealt with (though this is usually less immediate than with ACOs who deal with them as and when they arise).

Keeping records of decisions

Whatever method is used to manage cases, all outcomes should be recorded and the reasons for decisions shared with students. There are legal requirements to do so (Hart, 2001) but more importantly, record keeping can contribute to institutional development by enabling more detailed monitoring of outcomes. In my own institution, annual reports that go to university committees and other interested parties have been instrumental in guiding the development of assessments and shaping course design to address some of the things that the data shows might need attention. To allow for this kind of evaluation, you will need records with sufficient detail and a designated person with responsibility to inspect them. Where this happens, institutions find it useful to look out for:

- inconsistencies in the application of the procedures between academic areas;

- areas where teaching of correct attribution could be strengthened;

- groups of students who are particularly vulnerable to misunderstanding attribution conventions; and

- common errors in attribution.

Have students been told?

The point being made here is not how, when or where students are told about academic integrity; it is whether or not the institution makes any effort to check it happens as part of normal quality assurance and/or if efforts to inform students have been successful. Admittedly, it is hard to be sure of students' understanding as many are not interested in the matter until it happens to them. Publicising penalties might encourage student interest, but whatever approach is adopted, students should never be given reason to believe that, because the lecturer has not told them that work will be checked, they can cheat with impunity.

Similarly, students should know if the lecturer is taking active steps to check the authenticity of student work by electronic screening. Random or partial checks are a legitimate adjunct to normal academic judgement. Such actions must be explained with care or years of effort to create an atmosphere of collegial working between staff and students might be put at risk. It seems likely that the relative novelty of electronic detection means good practice about informing students is still developing.

Clear roles and responsibilities

The many people responsible for operationalising a policy will need their roles spelled out in the procedures. An example of a policy which does this was described by Park (2004) and the online version includes some roles specific to the University of Lancaster where this version was ratified

(www.lancs.ac.uk/users/celt/plagiarism/plagiarism_summary.doc).

At a minimum, your own version will need to specify:

- The **individual marker's** responsibilities. These should include using a range of strategies for detecting plagiarism; producing grounds for identifying the work as plagiarised; providing information to relevant officers; and ensuring actions are completed within a short space of time.

- The **course leader's** responsibilities. These will include ensuring all students are aware of procedures and requirements for attribution; and ensuring all markers use consistent means for identifying plagiarism.

- A named **convenor of regular meetings** with specialist officers. Unless these people meet regularly, exchange ideas and discuss their practice, they will become more and more individualistic in their decisions, losing the benefits of consistency and shared practice. Meetings need to occur several times a year and be long enough to allow discussion and consensus to develop.

- A named person, perhaps the convener, responsible for **inducting** newly appointed specialists and ensuring they build on previous shared experience.

- A named person responsible for **informing and consulting staff and students** about the institution's policies and procedures. Someone should also be charged with collecting and making sense of accumulating data on incidence, punishments, and evolving practice, usually as part of the university's quality enhancement process.

Publicising the policy change

Once agreed (and this often takes a surprisingly long time), a policy needs to be ratified then widely circulated and publicised. If a project group has managed the project and consulted widely, then the new version should not come as a surprise, but it often takes careful planning to ensure everyone knows about it. Briefings should be tailored to the recipients' need to know relevant procedures. When planning briefings, think beyond teaching staff to include librarians, registry administrators, students and student union advocates. Groups with specific responsibilities will also need to know about changes so include briefings for course committees, departmental management boards and staff unions. Finally, any new staff will need to be told as part of their induction, just as each new student cohort will need the message as part of theirs. Since knowledge and understanding fade quickly, updates will be necessary, too.

A co-ordinated strategy against plagiarism

However workable the procedures and however carefully drafted the wording, a policy will sit unread and unused in the handbook unless steps are taken to make it live. This inevitably entails moving beyond generic support ('The university is committed to the integrity of its awards', 'Academic integrity is at the heart of all we do'). By publicising activity rather than keeping it secret as apparently was the norm even a few years ago, senior managers are likely to improve rather than threaten the institution's reputation. They will show their commitment by:

- **Allocating appropriate resources**, usually in the form of people's time.

- Ensuring **access to support and specialist advice**. Again, time is a key feature since expertise in areas such as electronic text-matching, course/assessment design and teaching academic writing skills do not develop quickly or spontaneously.

- Ensuring **staff development** where it is needed.

- Encouraging **measures for embedding practice**. Tackling academic misconduct will always remain a reactive process unless institutions integrate their development of methods for tackling academic misconduct relating to course design, teaching and assessment into the existing and normal course review and quality assurance procedures. Of course, additional resources to encourage implementation in the early stages may be necessary.

Plagiarism Awareness week at the University of Sussex

The catchphrase: 'Spend ten minutes on plagiarism this week'.

The aims: To educate students, promote discussion and help people find out about resources and support.

The activities: Teaching Staff to lead a 10-minute presentation/discussion. (There's a generic PowerPoint for staff to edit and adapt.) Students to complete an online tutorial devised by a Canadian university (http://library.acadiau.ca /tutorials/plagiarism/) then check out the university's own site. The Students' Union: an online discussion forum.

- Setting **targets and timetables**. Public statements about realistic targets and action plans for achieving them will significantly aid progress. However, in order to set realistic targets it is likely that there will have to be some initial research to establish the current extent and nature of academic misconduct. This will require resources.

- Creating **a procedure for reviewing progress**. This needs to be done on a regular basis, and the various aspects of the policy amended as appropriate.

Whilst the above section sets out the necessary components for institutional progress, the speed of change may well depend upon the appearance of enthusiasts and champions. Such individuals cannot be compelled into existence, but most institutions have people who are interested in plagiarism, in electronic detection and in teaching students the requisite skills. The skill of a committed senior management will lie in identifying, encouraging and supporting such individuals if and when they appear.

References

Angelil-Carter, S. (2000), 'Understanding plagiarism differently', in Leibowitz, B. and Mohammed, Y. (eds.), *Routes to Writing in Southern Africa* (Cape Town: Silk Road International Publishers).

Austin, Z., Simpson, S., and Reynen, E. (2005), 'The fault lies not in our students, but in ourselves: academic honesty and moral development in health professions education – results of a pilot study in Canadian pharmacy', *Teaching in Higher Education*, 10:2, 143-56.

Bannister, P. and Ashworth, P. (1998), 'Four good reasons for cheating and plagiarism', in Rust, C. (ed.), *Improving Student Learning Symposium* (Oxford: Oxford Centre for Staff and Learning Development, Oxford Brookes University), 233-241.

Barnett, R. and Cox, A. (2005), 'At least they are learning something: the hazy line between collaboration and collusion', *Assessment and Evaluation in Higher Education*, 30:2, 107-22.

Bennett, R. (2005), 'Factors associated with student plagiarism in a post-1992 university', *Assessment and Evaluation in Higher Education*, 30:2, 137-162.

Biggs, J. (1999), *Teaching for Quality Learning in Higher Education*, p. 129 quoting Wilson, 1997, (Milton Keynes: Open University).

Boehm, D. (1998), 'About plagiarism, pixels and platitudes', http://kairos.technorhetoric.net/3.1/coverweb/boehm/pixels.htm.

Bull, J., Collins, C., Coughlin, E., and Sharpe, D. (2001), 'Technical review of plagiarism detection software report', http://www.jiscpas.ac.uk/uploaded_documents/luton.pdf.

Burkhill, S. and Franklyn-Stokes, A. (2004), 'Empowering your students to avoid plagiarism', in Peden Smith, A. and Duggan, F. (eds.), *Plagiarism Prevention, Practice and Policy Conference Proceedings, 28-30 June 2004*, (Newcastle: Northumbria University Press), 291-295.

Carroll, J. (2002), 'Deterring student plagiarism: where best to start?', in Rust, C. (ed.), *Improving Student Learning Symposium* (Oxford: Oxford Centre for Staff and Learning Development, Oxford Brookes University)

Carroll, J. and Appleton, J. (2001), *Plagiarism: A Good Practice Guide*, available at http://www.jiscpas.ac.uk.

Carroll, J. and Appleton, J. (2005), 'Towards consistent penalty decisions for breaches of academic regulations in one UK university', *International Journal for Educational Integrity*, 1:1, http://www.ojs.unisa.edu.au/journals/index.php/IJEI/issue/current.

Carroll, J. and Duggan, F. (2005), 'Institutional change as part of a holistic approach to deterring student plagiarism: a comparative survey', in *Conference Proceedings, Educational Integrity: Values in Teaching, Learning and Research*, 2-3 December 2005, (University of Newcastle, Australia).

Carroll, J. and Ryan, J. (2005), *Teaching International Students: Improving Learning for All*, (London: Routledge).

Carroll, J. and Seymour, D. (2006), 'The effect of a penalty tariff on consistent decision-making in cases of student plagiarism', *Proceedings of the 2nd International Plagiarism Conference*, 19-21 June 2006, (Newcastle, UK).

CAVAL Collaborative Solutions (2002), *Victorian Vice-Chancellors' Electronic Plagiarism Detection Pilot Project: Member Project Report* (Melbourne: CAVAL Collaborative Solutions), September 2002.

Chester, G. (2001), 'Plagiarism detection and prevention: final report of the JISC electronic plagiarism detection project', http://www.jisc.ac.uk/uploaded_documents/plagiarism_final.pdf.

Cogdell, R., Matthew, R. and Gray, C. (2002), 'Academic cheating: an investigation of medical students' views on cheating in a problem-based learning course', in Rust, C. (ed.), *Improving Student Learning Symposium* (Oxford: Oxford Centre for Staff and Learning Development, Oxford Brookes University).

Cole, S. and Kiss, E. (2000), 'What can we do about student cheating?', *About Campus*, May-June 2000, 5-12.

Cox, A., Currall, J., and Connolly, S. (2001), 'The human and organisational issues associated with network security', http://litc.sbu.ac.uk/jcalt.

Culwin, F. (2006), 'Either my students are getting naughtier, or the tools are getting better!', in *Proceedings of the 2nd International Plagiarism Conference*, 19-21 June 2006, (Newcastle, UK).

Culwin, F. and Lancaster, T. (2001), 'Plagiarism prevention and detection', http://cise.sbu.ac.uk.

Culwin, F., MacLeod, A., and Lancaster, T. (2001), 'Source code plagiarism in UK HE computing schools: issues, attitudes and tools', http://www.jiscpas.ac.uk/pub01/southbank.pdf.

Davies, P. (2004), 'Don't write, just mark: the validity of assessing student ability via their computerized peer-marking of an essay rather than their creation of an essay', *Research in Learning Technology*, 12:3, 261-277.

Deech, R. (2004), 'Annual report of the Office of Independent Adjudicator for Higher Education', http://www.oiahe.org.uk/docs/OIA-Annual-Report-2004.pdf.

Deech, R. (2006), Keynote address, in *Proceedings of the 2nd International Plagiarism Conference*, 19-21 June 2006, (Newcastle, UK).

Devlin, M. (2003), 'The problem with plagiarism', *Campus Review*, 12:44, 4-5.

Errey, L. (2001), 'Something fishy…or just a fish out of water?', *Teaching Forum*, 50, 17-20.

Evans, J. (2000), 'Autoplagiarism', *Educational Technology News*, Summer 2000, 12.

Fox, H. (1994), *Listening to the World: Cultural Issues in Academic Writing* (Urbana, Illinois: National Council of Teachers of English).

Franklyn-Stokes, A. and Newstead, S. E. (1995), 'Undergraduate cheating: who does what and why', *Studies in Higher Education*, 20:2, 159-172.

Freewood, M. (2001), 'Student perceptions of plagiarism: a research project', Sheffield Hallam University Plagiarism and Inappropriate Collusion Steering Group.

Freewood, M., Macdonald, R. and Ashworth, P. (2003), 'Why simply policing plagiarism is not the answer', in Rust, C. (ed.), *Improving Student Learning Theory and Practice – 10 Years On* (Oxford: Oxford Centre for Staff and Learning Development, Oxford Brookes University).

FreshMinds (June, 2004) *Plagiarism Survey*, http://www.freshminds.co.uk/FreshMinds/plagiarism_survey.pdf.

Fritz, C., Morris, P., Bjork, R., Gelman, R., and Wickens, T. (2000), 'When learning fails: stability and change following repeated presentation of text', *Journal of Psychology*, 91:4, 493-511.

Furedi, F. (2000), 'On-line cat and mouse', *Times Higher Education Supplement*, 14 July 2000.

Gajadhar, J. (1998), 'Issues in plagiarism for the new millennium: an assessment odyssey', http://ultibase.rmit.edu.au/Articles/dec98/gajad1.htm.

Grafen, A. (2006), 'Plagiarism at Oxford' *Oxford Magazine*, No. 249, 16–18.

Graham, A. and Leung, C. (2004), 'Uncovering "blind spots": culture and copying', in Peden Smith, A. and Duggan, F. (eds.), *Plagiarism Prevention, Practice and Policy Conference Proceedings*, 28-30 June 2004 (Newcastle: Northumbria University Press), 73-83.

Grossman, W. (2002), 'All their own work?', *The Independent*, 15 April 2002.

Hanlon, W. (2002), 'Sharpening students' analytical skills', in *Focus on University Teaching and Learning*, 11:3 (Dalhousie University).

Harris, R. (2001), 'Anti-plagiarism strategies in research papers', http://www.virtualsalt.com/antiplag.htm.

Hinchcliffe, L. (1998), 'Cut and paste plagiarism: preventing, detecting and tracking online plagiarism', http://www.uregina-ca/tdc/CutPastePlagiarism-htm.

Hunt, R. (2004), 'Whose silverware is this? Promoting plagiarism through pedagogy (or Peter Piper picked a peck of purloined passages)', in Peden Smith, A. and Duggan, F. (eds.), *Plagiarism Prevention, Practice and Policy Conference Proceedings*, 28-30 June 2004 (Newcastle:Northumbria University Press), 265-275.

Lambert, K., Ellen, N., and Taylor, L. (2006), 'Chalkface challenges: a study of academic dishonesty amongst students in New Zealand tertiary institutions', *Assessment and Evaluation in Higher Education*, 31:5, 485-503.

Larkham, P. and Manns, S. (2002), 'Plagiarism and its treatment in higher education', *Journal of Further and Higher Education*, 26:4, 341-49.

Levin, P. (2004), 'Beat the witch-hunt! Peter Levin's guide to avoiding and rebutting accusations of plagiarism, for conscientious students', http://www.student-friendly-guides.com/plagiarism/beat_the_witch-hunt.pdf.

Levin, P. (2006), 'Why the writing is on the wall for the plagiarism police', http://www.student-friendly-guides.com/plagiarism/writing_on_the_wall.pdf.

McCabe, D. (2003), 'Promoting academic integrity: a US/Canadian perspective', in *Proceedings of the First Australian Educational Integrity Conference*, 21-22 November 2003, (University of South Australia), 3-11.

McCabe, D. and Trevino, L. (2002), 'Honesty and honor codes', *Academe*, 88:1, 37-41.

McDowell, L. and Brown, S. (2001), 'Assessing students: cheating and plagiarism', http://www.heacademy.ac.uk/embedded_object.asp?id=21639&filename=McDowell_and_Brown.

McKenzie, J. (1998), 'The new plagiarism: seven antidotes to prevent highway robbery in an electronic age', http://fno.org/may98/cov98may.html.

Macdonald, R. (2000), 'Why don't we turn the tide of plagiarism to the learner's advantage?', *Times Higher Education Supplement*, 24 November 2000.

Macdonald, R. and Carroll, J. (2006), 'Plagiarism – a complex issue requiring a holistic institutional approach', *Assessment and Evaluation in Higher Education*, 31:2, 233-245.

Maslen, G. (2003), '80% admit to cheating', *Times Higher Education Supplement*, 23 January 2003.

Mirow, M. and Shore, P. (1997), 'Plagiarism and textual ownership in a digital source environment', *Proteus: A Journal of Ideas*, 14:1, 41-43.

Olsel, V. (1998), 'Jane Eyre to go', *Salon Magazine*, http://www.salon.com/it/career/1998/11/13career.html.

Park, C. (2003), 'In other (people's) words: plagiarism by university students – literature and lessons', *Assessment and Evaluation in Higher Education,* 28:5, 471-488.

Park, C. (2004), 'Rebels without a clause: towards an institutional framework for dealing with plagiarism by students', *Journal of Further and Higher Education,* 28:3, 291-306.

Peverett, C. (2004), cited in Lambert et al. (2006), 'Chalkface challenges: a study of academic dishonesty amongst students in New Zealand tertiary institutions', *Assessment and Evaluation in Higher Education*, 31:5, 485-503.

Roig, M. and deTommasco, L. (1995), 'Are college cheating and plagiarism related to academic procrastination?', *Psychological Reports*, 77, 691-98.

Rust, C. (2001), 'A briefing on assessment of large groups' in *LTSN Generic Centre Assessment Series,* http://www.business.heacademy.ac.uk/resources/landt/assess/group.pdf.

Ryan, J. (2000), *A Guide to Teaching International Students* (Oxford: Oxford Centre for Staff and Learning Development, Oxford Brookes University).

Schmitt, D. (2005), 'Writing in the international classroom', in Carroll, J. and Ryan, J. (eds.), *Teaching International Students: Improving Learning for All* (London: Routledge), 63-75.

Schott, G. (2003), 'The reference: more than a buttress of the scientific edifice', *The Journal of the Royal Society of Medicine*, 96, 191-193.

Seymour, D. (2006), 'Students' attitudes towards cheating in University Education', *Proceedings of the CHME 2006 Research Conference* (Nottingham: CHME).

Shi, L. (2004), 'Textual borrowing in second-language writing', *Written Communication*, 2:2, 171-200.

Simon, C., Carr, J., McCullough, S., Morgan, S., Oleson, T., and Ressel, M. (2003), 'The other side of academic dishonesty: the relationship between scepticism, gender and strategies for managing student academic dishonesty cases', *Assessment and Evaluation in Higher Education*, 28:2, 193-207.

Simon, C., Carr, J., McCullough, S., Morgan, S., Oleson, T. and Ressel, M. (2004), 'Gender, student perceptions, institutional commitments and academic dishonesty: who reports in academic dishonesty cases?', *Assessment and Evaluation in Higher Education*, 29:1, 75-90.

Swales, J. and Feak, C. (1994), *Academic Writing for Graduate Students* (Ann Arbor: University of Michigan).

Szabo, A. and Underwood, J. (2004), 'Cybercheats: is information and communication technology fuelling academic dishonesty?', *Active Learning in Higher Education*, 5:2, 180-199.

Taylor, M. and Butt, R. (2006), 'Q: How do you make £1.6m a year and drive a Ferrari? A: Sell essays for £400', *The Guardian*, 29 July 2006.

Volet, S. and Kee, J. (1993), 'Studying in Singapore – Studying in Australia', *Murdoch University Teaching Excellence Series*, Occasional Paper 1.

Wahrer, S. (2002), 'Plagiarism: avoiding the greatest academic sin', http:www.bgsu.edu/offices/acen/writerslab/handouts/plagiarism.pdf.

Walker, J. (1998), 'Student plagiarism in universities: what are we doing about it?', *Higher Education Research and Development*, 17:1, 89-106.

Watkins, J. and Biggs, J. (1996), *The Chinese Learner* (Hong Kong: Comparative Education Research Centre).

Wilson, K. (1997), 'Wording it up: plagiarism and the interdiscourse of international students', paper given to the annual conference, Higher Education Research and Development Society of Australia, Adelaide, 8-11 July.

Yeo, S. and Chien, R. (2005), 'The seriousness of plagiarism incidents: making consistent decisions across a university', paper given to the Asia Pacific Educational Integrity Conference, Newcastle, Australia, December, 2005, http://www.newcastle.edu.au/conference/apeic/papers.html.